When students have difficulty applying a strategy or skill, an array of multisensory teaching strategies is available to help you modify your methods and accommodate students' needs.

RETEACH LESSONS

GRAMMAR RETEACH

Kinds of Sentences

OBJECTIVE: *To recognize and use different kinds of sentences*

Focus

Share the following information with students.

> A *sentence* must express a complete thought, and the words in a sentence must be in logical order. All sentences begin with capital letters and end with end marks. A *statement* tells something and ends with a period. A *question* asks something and ends with a question mark. An *exclamation* expresses strong emotion and ends with an exclamation mark. A *command* gives an order and ends with a period or an exclamation point. Knowing the different types of sentences helps readers understand the stories and articles they read.

Choose a Teaching Model

VISUAL MODEL Write the following matching diagram on the board, omitting the connecting lines and end punctuation.

Sentences	Descriptions
My great-grandmother planted that tree.	asks a question
Have you ever seen such a lovely maple tree?	gives a command
Be careful if you are going to climb it.	makes an exclamation
What huge leaves it has!	makes a statement

Read the sentences aloud to students. Then tell students to copy the diagram onto a sheet of paper. Have students identify the sentence types by drawing lines between the sentences in the left-hand column and the descriptions in the right-hand column. Then have students work in pairs to add the correct end mark to each sentence. Ask volunteers to transfer their answers to the diagram on the board. Then follow the suggestions in **Summarize/Reinforce.**

AUDITORY MODEL Duplicate the diagram from the Visual Model, omitting the connecting lines and end punctuation. Distribute the diagram to pairs of students. Have students take turns reading the sentences aloud. The listener should identify each sentence as a statement, question, exclamation, or command. Then ask students the following questions: "Which sentence should end with an exclamation point? A period? A question mark? A period or an exclamation point?" Ask volunteers to answer the questions orally as all students add the correct end marks to the sentences. Then follow the suggestions in **Summarize/Reinforce.**

KINESTHETIC/MOTOR MODEL Display in two columns the sentences and phrases from the diagram in the Visual Model. Omit the connecting lines and end punctuation. Read aloud the two columns, and have students work in pairs to copy them. Then have partners circle the matching sentences and phrases using a different-colored marker or crayon for each matching pair. Next, draw on the board a period, a question mark, and an exclamation point. Ask volunteers to circle the end mark on the board that belongs at the end of each sentence using the same color marker. Then follow the suggestions in **Summarize/Reinforce.**

Summarize/Reinforce

Check students' understanding of the lesson by having them summarize what they learned. (A sentence must be a complete thought and the words must be in logical order. A statement tells something and ends with a period. A question asks something and ends with a question mark. An exclamation expresses strong emotion and ends with an exclamation mark. A command gives an order and ends with a period or an exclamation point.) You may want to reinforce the lesson by having students find examples of each sentence type in a story they have read. Remind students to use the information from this lesson to help them understand the kinds of sentences they come across as they read.

COMPREHENSION RETEACH

Cause and Effect

OBJECTIVE: *To determine cause-and-effect relationships*

Focus

Share the following information with students:

> **The reason something happens is the *cause*. What happens is the *effect*. Clue words such as *because*, *so*, and *as a result* may signal causes and effects. An effect can have more than one cause, and a cause can be stated or unstated.**

Choose a Teaching Model

VISUAL MODEL Display or duplicate the following chart, leaving space for the answers:

Cause Why Something Happened	Effect What Happened
(There was a large patch of colorful lupines on the other side of the hill.)	Alice cried, "I don't believe my eyes!" when she walked over the hill.
Alice decided that the park conservatory was like a tropical isle, but not quite.	(Alice went to a real tropical island.)
(Alice admired her grandfather and wanted to be like him.)	Alice went to faraway places and lived by the sea, just as her grandfather had done.

Discuss the chart with students. Guide students to ask "What happened?" and "Why did it happen?" to figure out what goes in each blank. Students may reread passages from the selection that give information about these relationships. When the chart is complete, have students use the information and clue words such as *because, so,* and *as a result* to write cause-and-effect sentences. Then follow the suggestions in **Summarize/Reinforce.**

AUDITORY MODEL Read aloud each cause or effect provided in the chart in the Visual Model, asking volunteers to supply the missing cause or effect. If necessary, read aloud the story passages that give information about these relationships, emphasizing clue words. Have students make up other sentences that state cause-and-effect relationships and share them with the group. Then follow the suggestions in **Summarize/Reinforce.**

KINESTHETIC/MOTOR MODEL Distribute copies of the chart in the Visual Model, showing the causes and effects scrambled within each column. Have students draw lines linking the effects with their causes. Next, have volunteers read the results aloud. Then follow the suggestions in **Summarize/Reinforce.**

Summarize/Reinforce

Have students summarize what they learned. (Asking "What happened?" and "Why did it happen?" helps readers figure out causes and effects. Authors may use clue words to show a cause-and-effect relationship. There may be more than one cause. A cause may be stated or unstated.) You may want to reinforce the lesson by having students identify cause-and-effect relationships in other selections. Remind them to use the strategies from this lesson to help them better understand what they read.

COMPREHENSION STRATEGY
RETEACH

Active Reading Strategies

OBJECTIVE: *To apply reading process strategies to gain meaning*

Focus

Share the following information with students:

Reading strategies **are plans readers can use to make sure they understand what they are reading. Before reading, readers should preview, predict what will happen, and set a purpose for reading. During reading, readers should use context clues to figure out the meaning of unfamiliar words, reread, summarize, and check or change the predictions made before reading. After reading, readers should decide whether the purpose for reading was met and whether they enjoyed the story. Knowing when to use each of the reading strategies helps readers better understand what they read.**

Choose a Teaching Model

VISUAL MODEL Print three column headings on the board: *Before Reading, During Reading, After Reading.* Then write the following strategies on individual index cards:

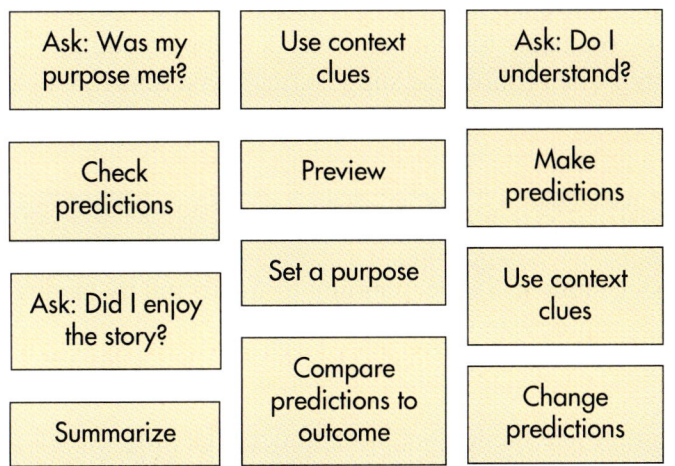

Display the cards in random order. Call on students, one at a time, to go to the front, select a strategy card, and explain or demonstrate how the strategy is used. Have students tape the strategy cards under the correct headings on the board. Remind students that some strategies, such as making and confirming predictions, are used before, during, and after reading. Have students copy the completed chart onto drawing paper and decorate the chart with colored pencils or markers. Suggest that students refer to their charts when reading. Then follow the suggestions in **Summarize/Reinforce.**

AUDITORY MODEL Hold up a fiction book students have read, and ask questions such as these: "Who can name a strategy we can use *before* reading this story? Who can name a reason why we might like to read this story? Who can suggest a strategy you could use if you were confused while you were reading? What can you do *after* reading to help you remember this story?" Have students answer these questions orally. Repeat the process with a nonfiction book. Then follow the suggestions in **Summarize/Reinforce.**

KINESTHETIC/MOTOR MODEL Copy the list of strategies from the Visual Model onto the board. Give each student several strips of three different colors of paper. Have students list the Before Reading strategies on a strip of one color, the During Reading strategies on another color, and the After Reading strategies on the third color. Remind students that some strategies are used before, during, and after reading. Have students place each strip in a book or story at the point where the strategy is used. Encourage students to explain where and why they placed various strips. Then follow the suggestions in **Summarize/Reinforce.**

Summarize/Reinforce

Check students' understanding of the lesson by having them summarize what they learned. (Previewing, predicting, and setting a purpose are Before Reading strategies. Using context clues, rereading, summarizing, and checking or changing predictions are During Reading strategies. After reading, students can decide whether they liked the story, whether they met their purposes for reading, and whether their predictions were correct.) You may want to reinforce the lesson by having students discuss the strategies they use as they read another story.

A PLACE TO DREAM

RETEACH LESSONS / R5

GRAMMAR RETEACH

Parts of a Sentence: Subject

OBJECTIVE: *To identify and use subjects*

Focus

Share the following with students:

Every sentence has a *subject* that tells who or what the sentence is about. The subject usually appears at the beginning of a sentence. Being able to identify the subject of a sentence can help readers understand what they read.

Choose a Teaching Model

VISUAL MODEL Write the following sentences on the board:

1. **The pioneer family built a new barn.**
2. **The nearby forest provided them with wood.**
3. **Neighbors arrived to help them.**
4. **The huge barn took many days to complete.**

Below the sentences complete a web with students, similar to the one shown. Ask volunteers to identify the subject in each sentence. Add each subject to the web as it is identified.

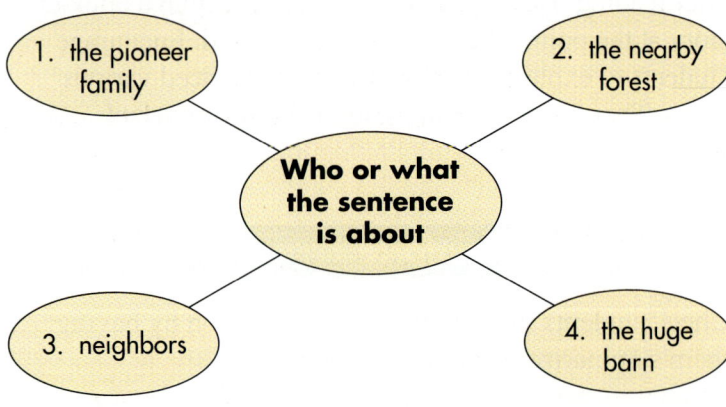

Write these sentence frames on the board:

_____ **helped build the new barn.**

_____ **planted an apple orchard.**

_____ **was home to many wild animals.**

_____ **was built in three days.**

Have students first work in pairs to copy each sentence frame and then to complete it by adding one of the subjects from the web. Remind students to begin their sentences with a capital letter. Ask volunteers to share their sentences and identify the subjects. Then follow the suggestions in **Summarize/Reinforce**.

AUDITORY MODEL Display the sentences from the Visual Model, and read them aloud. Read them a second time, more slowly, and have students raise their hands when they hear the subject of each sentence. Ask volunteers to underline the subjects. Have students work in pairs to write two sentences about a person, place, or thing they might find near a pioneer's home. Then have partners write their sentences on the board. Ask partners to orally identify the subject in each other's sentence. Then follow the suggestions in **Summarize/Reinforce**.

KINESTHETIC/MOTOR MODEL Display the sentences from the Visual Model, and read them aloud. Have volunteers underline the subject in each sentence. Next, have students work in pairs. Each partner should list at least three people, places, or things that might be found near a pioneer's home. Have partners exchange lists and write sentences using each other's words as the subject. Have partners exchange lists again and check each other's work. Ask volunteers to share their sentences by reading them aloud. Then follow the suggestions in **Summarize/ Reinforce**.

Summarize/Reinforce

Check students' understanding of the lesson by having them summarize what they learned. (The subject of a sentence tells who or what the sentence is about. The subject is usually found in the beginning of a sentence.) To reinforce the lesson, have students identify the subject in sentences from other stories they have read. Remind students to use the information in this lesson to help them write more clearly and better understand what they read.

STUDY SKILLS RETEACH

Following Directions

OBJECTIVE: *To interpret and follow directions*

Focus

Share the following information with students:

Knowing how to understand and *follow directions* can help readers do many things. To follow directions, read them or listen to them carefully; gather materials; ask questions if something is unclear; use pictures or diagrams to follow each step in order.

Choose a Teaching Model

VISUAL MODEL Explain that students are going to follow directions to make a time line of Johnny Appleseed's life. Display or duplicate the directions below and have students read them silently:

Making a Time Line

Things you will need: a sheet of drawing paper, a pen or pencil, a ruler, the selection "Johnny Appleseed"

1. At the top of your paper, write *A Time Line of Johnny Appleseed's Life.*
2. Draw a four-inch horizontal line on the paper.
3. At the beginning of the line, draw a circle. Write the year Johnny was born below the circle.
4. At the other end of the line, make another circle. Below it, write the year Johnny died.
5. Above the time line, write one important thing that happened in Johnny's life. Mark the time line to show about when this happened.

Allow time for students to ask questions. Then invite volunteers to describe in their own words what they need to do. If necessary, students may look back through the selection to help them locate important dates and events. Have students follow the directions, and then ask them why it was important to follow the directions in order. Then follow the suggestions in **Summarize/Reinforce.**

AUDITORY MODEL Ask students to listen carefully as you read aloud the set of directions used in the Visual Model. Pause after you read the list of materials to allow time for students to gather materials and then continue reading the directions. Read aloud all of the directions. Give students an opportunity to ask questions. Then reread each numbered step, and pause as students complete it. When students have finished, ask them to use their completed time lines to review events in Johnny Appleseed's life. Then follow the suggestions in **Summarize/Reinforce.**

KINESTHETIC/MOTOR MODEL Duplicate the directions from the Visual Model and give each student a copy. Have students read through the directions. Then ask them to point to such things as the list of materials needed, the steps of directions, the first step, and the last step.

Next, have students follow the directions and share their results. Then follow the suggestions in **Summarize/ Reinforce.**

Summarize/Reinforce

Have students summarize what they learned. (To follow directions, carefully read or listen to each step. Gather materials. Ask questions if you do not understand, use pictures or diagrams to follow the steps in the correct order.) To reinforce the lesson, have students work in pairs to follow other directions for doing something. Remind students to use the strategies from this lesson when they need to follow directions.

VOCABULARY STRATEGY
RETEACH

Structural and Contextual Clues

OBJECTIVE: *To use structural and contextual clues to determine meanings of words*

Focus

Share the following information with students:

When readers come across an unfamiliar word, they can use *context clues* and *word structure* to figure out the meaning of the word. Context clues are meaning clues given by the other words and sentences that surround an unfamiliar word. Word structure is the way a word is put together. Knowing how to use structural and contextual clues to figure out word meanings helps readers understand what they read.

Choose a Teaching Model

VISUAL MODEL Display the following passage:

> **The dog bolted <u>eagerly</u> toward the squirrel. The squirrel scampered to the <u>treetop</u>. "I was <u>unable</u> to make friends with the squirrel," he sighed to himself. "I guess I'll <u>return</u> tomorrow."**

Have students read the passage silently and look for structural and contextual clues to help them figure out the meaning of each underlined word. Draw the following chart on the board, and write the underlined words in the first column.

Word	Context Clues or Word Part Clues	Meaning
eagerly	*eager* means "impatient and excited" *-ly* means "in a way that is"	"in a way that is impatient and excited"

Model how to figure out the meaning of *eagerly* by circling the base word *eager* and underlining the suffix *-ly*. Write the meanings of the word parts in the middle column. Then help students figure out what the word means, and write the meaning in the third column. Have pairs of students copy the chart onto a separate sheet of paper and work together to find meaning clues for the other words. Then follow the suggestions in **Summarize/Reinforce**.

AUDITORY MODEL Read the passage from the Visual Model aloud. Then display the chart. Model how to use word parts to figure out the meaning of *eagerly* by circling the word parts and explaining their meaning. Record this information on the chart. Then have students work in pairs to copy the chart and to find and record the other word part clues, context clues, and word meanings. Then follow the suggestions in **Summarize/Reinforce**.

KINESTHETIC/MOTOR MODEL Distribute a copy of the passage from the Visual Model to each student. Display the following word meanings on the board: "in a way that is impatient and excited"; "the top of a tree"; "not able to do something"; "come back." Have students copy these meanings onto their papers. Demonstrate how to use word part clues to figure out the meaning of *eagerly*. Have each student circle the base word *eager* and underline the suffix *-ly*. Then have them circle the base words *able* and *turn* and underline the prefixes *un-* and *re-*. Also have them underline meaning clues in a different color and circle the two words that make up *treetop*. Finally, have them draw a line from each underlined word to its meaning. Discuss with students how they used clues to figure out word meanings. Then follow the suggestions in **Summarize/Reinforce**.

Summarize/Reinforce

Check students' understanding of the lesson by having them summarize what they learned. (Structural and contextual clues can help readers figure out the meanings of unfamiliar words.) For reinforcement, have students read a nonfiction article and use the strategies in this lesson to decode unfamiliar words.

**GRAMMAR
RETEACH**

Parts of a Sentence: Predicate

OBJECTIVE: *To identify and use predicates*

Focus

Share the following with students:

> **In order to tell a complete thought, a sentence must contain a subject and a *predicate*. The predicate usually appears in the last part of a sentence and tells what the subject of the sentence is or does.**

Choose a Teaching Model

VISUAL MODEL Display the following sentences on the board:

- **The apartment building was sixty feet tall.**
- **My friend and I raced up four flights of stairs.**
- **We were out of breath!**
- **Katie pointed out the window.**
- **We looked at the people far below.**

Have students copy the sentences onto a sheet of paper and draw a box around the predicate in each sentence. Model this by drawing a box around the predicate in the first sentence. Have volunteers identify the subject and predicate in each sentence on the board. Then ask pairs of students to write five new sentences, using the same subjects but different predicates. Have volunteers write their sentences on the board. Finally, ask other volunteers to draw boxes around the new predicates. Then follow the suggestions in **Summarize/Reinforce**.

AUDITORY MODEL Display the sentences from the Visual Model. Ask pairs of volunteers to read the sentences aloud, one partner reading the subject and the other reading the predicate. Model this process with a volunteer. Underline the predicate in each sentence as it is read. Next, have students work in pairs to write two sentences that describe what they might see or do in a city like New York. Have partners share their sentences by writing them on the board and reading them aloud, using the format described above. Then follow the suggestions in **Summarize/Reinforce**.

KINESTHETIC/MOTOR MODEL Display the sentences from the Visual Model. Have pairs of students copy each sentence onto a separate strip of paper. Then have them separate each sentence into the subject and the predicate by cutting the strip in two. Model identifying subject and predicate, using the first sentence as an example. Have partners glue all the subjects onto a sheet of paper under the heading *Subjects* and the corresponding predicates under the heading *Predicates*. Have partners exchange their lists with another pair to check each other's work. Then follow the suggestions in **Summarize/Reinforce**.

Summarize/Reinforce

Check students' understanding of the lesson by having them summarize what they learned. (Every sentence has a predicate. A predicate tells what the subject is or does. The predicate usually appears at the end of the sentence.) You may want to reinforce the lesson by having students identify the predicates in sentences from a story they have read recently.

STUDY SKILLS RETEACH

Alphabetical Order

OBJECTIVE: *To alphabetize using the fourth and fifth letters*

Focus

Share the following information with students:

To put two words in *alphabetical order*, begin by looking at the first letter in each word. If this letter is the same in both words, look at the second letter. If the second and third letters of the words are the same, use the fourth letter to alphabetize. If the fourth is the same, use the fifth. Alphabetical order can help you find names in a telephone book and find words and topics in dictionaries, encyclopedias, card files, and other information sources.

Choose a Teaching Model

VISUAL MODEL Display the diagram below:

1	2	3	4	5	
J	e	s	s	e	
J	e	s	s	i	ca
J	e	s	s	a	mine

Point out that the first four letters of the three names are the same. Have students read the names and decide which letter column they would use to put the names in alphabetical order. (the fifth column) Then ask a volunteer to write the names in alphabetical order on the board. Next, display the lists below. Have pairs of students use the diagram to rewrite each list in alphabetical order.

Maria	Samantha	Carla
Mark	Samuel	Carlos
Marcos	Sammy	Carlin

Ask volunteers to write their lists on the board and circle the letter they used in each word to alphabetize the list. Discuss with students how alphabetical order can help them use guide words in reference books. Then follow the suggestions in **Summarize/Reinforce.**

AUDITORY MODEL Display and read aloud the diagram from the Visual Model. Ask volunteers to tell which letters in the words in the diagram are the same, which letter in each word should be used to alphabetize the list, and then to read the list aloud in alphabetical order. Next, have pairs of students use the diagram to alphabetize the three lists from the Visual Model. Then ask the class to read their lists aloud chorally. Discuss with students which letters they used to alphabetize the lists and how to use alphabetical order when they are looking at guide words in reference books. Then follow the suggestions in **Summarize/Reinforce.**

KINESTHETIC/MOTOR MODEL Display the diagram from the Visual Model. Use a sheet of paper to cover up every letter except the first in each word. Then move the paper right, one letter at a time, and tell students to call "Stop!" when you have uncovered the letter in each word that should be used to alphabetize the list. Circle these letters and ask a volunteer to rewrite the list in alphabetical order. Next, distribute copies of the name lists from the Visual Model to pairs of students. Have the partners cut apart the names in each set and rearrange them in alphabetical order. Have students circle the letter in each word that helped them alphabetize the list. Finally, discuss how to use alphabetical order when looking at guide words in reference books. Then follow the suggestions in **Summarize/Reinforce.**

Summarize/Reinforce

Check students' understanding of the lesson by having them summarize what they learned. (To alphabetize a list of words, look at the first letters. If the second and third letters are the same, use the fourth to alphabetize the words. If the fourth letter is the same, use the fifth.) You may want to reinforce the lesson by having students look at how a column of words in the dictionary is alphabetized. Remind students to use what they learned in this lesson to help them find information in telephone books, dictionaries, and encyclopedias.

STUDY SKILLS
RETEACH

Sources of Information

OBJECTIVE: *To locate information in the library*

Focus

Share the following information with students:

To find books in a library we use the *card catalog*—an alphabetical set of cards or a computer database that contains information about the authors and the titles of all books, and subject cards for all nonfiction books. A subject card shows the subject, author, title, publisher, and copyright date. It also includes a *call number*—a series of letters and numbers that matches the series of letters and numbers on a library shelf. Reference books are special nonfiction books that may not be taken out of the library. Knowing how libraries are organized helps readers find the information they need.

Choose a Teaching Model

VISUAL MODEL Obtain sample catalog cards of fiction and nonfiction books. Have students work in groups of three to make colorful, poster-sized versions of title, subject, and author cards. Write the following labels on the board, and have groups add the appropriate labels to their posters: *title, author, subject, publisher, copyright date, call number*. Have students use the completed cards to help them write solutions to these problems:

1. I want to find a book titled *All About Birthdays*.
2. I want to find a book about birthdays, but I don't know the author or the title.
3. I want to find a book by my favorite author.

Ask volunteers to share their answers. Then follow the suggestions in **Summarize/Reinforce**.

AUDITORY MODEL Display the subject card below:

> BIRTHDAYS
> 977.26 Birdsall, Betty
> Birthday celebrations around the world/Betty Birdsall
> Toronto: June Press, ©1985

Read aloud and explain each part of the card. Then ask, "Who can tell me the call number? Where else is it found?" Repeat the procedure with the author, title, subject, publisher, and copyright date. Read aloud the three problems from the Visual Model. Have students work in pairs to read and solve the problems. Ask volunteers to share their answers. Then follow the suggestions in **Summarize/Reinforce**.

KINESTHETIC/MOTOR MODEL Duplicate the subject card from the Auditory Model, and give each student a copy. Have students point to the call number, subject, author, title, publisher, and copyright date as you name them. Then organize a library scavenger hunt. Have students write answers to a list of questions such as the following:

1. Find the *L* volume of an encyclopedia. What subject(s) can you read about on pages 50-51?
2. Find the call number for a book about soccer.
3. What is the title, author, publisher, copyright date, and call number of a book about dinosaurs? Locate this book on the shelf.
4. Find a fiction book by any author whose last name begins with the letter *B*. Write the title and the author's name.

Have a Reporter share their answers. Then follow the suggestions in **Summarize/Reinforce**.

Summarize/Reinforce

Check students' understanding of the lesson by having them summarize what they learned. (To find a book in a library, look for the title or author card in the card catalog or database. If the title and author of a nonfiction book are not known, use the subject card.) You may want to reinforce the lesson by having students go to the library and look for books on current social studies or science topics, or books by familiar authors. Remind students to use the information from the lesson to help them find library books and information quickly and easily.

A PLACE TO DREAM

GRAMMAR RETEACH

Common Nouns

OBJECTIVE: *To recognize and use common nouns*

Focus

Share the following with students:

A *common noun* names any person, place, or thing. A common noun begins with a lowercase letter. Knowing how to recognize common nouns helps readers better understand what they read.

Choose a Teaching Model

VISUAL MODEL Distribute the following paragraph, and read it aloud:

The boy walked from his house to the park. Along the way he waved to his friend. He sat on the grass beneath a tree. He brought his flute out and began to play. The birds whistled to his song. Then a girl walked over from the playground. She played along with him on her harmonica.

Tell students to find and list the common nouns in the paragraph. (*boy, friend, girl, house, park, playground, grass, tree, flute, birds, song, harmonica*) Suggest that they ask themselves whether each word names a person, place, or thing. Encourage students to think of more nouns. When students have finished, have volunteers take turns writing the nouns on the board. Remind students that common nouns should begin with lowercase letters. Then follow the suggestions in **Summarize/Reinforce**.

AUDITORY MODEL Distribute the paragraph from the Visual Model. Slowly read the paragraph aloud, and have students follow along silently. Read the paragraph a second time, and have students underline the common nouns. Have volunteers identify these nouns orally and state whether the noun names a person, a place, or a thing. List them on the board as they are named. Remind students that common nouns begin with lowercase letters. Then follow the suggestions in **Summarize/Reinforce**.

KINESTHETIC/MOTOR MODEL Create a stack of common-noun cards by writing one common noun on an index card for each student in the class. Use the common nouns from the paragraph in the Visual Model. Read the paragraph aloud, and as you come to a noun, pause for volunteers to hold up the correct card. Remind students that a common noun should begin with a lowercase letter. Then follow the suggestions in **Summarize/Reinforce**.

Summarize/Reinforce

Check students' understanding of the lesson by having them summarize what they learned. (*A common noun names any person, place, or thing. A common noun begins with a lowercase letter.*) You may want to reinforce this lesson by having students play "Twenty Questions." A student thinks of a common noun. Other students take turns asking questions requiring a *yes* or *no* response. The person who guesses the common noun gets to think of the next one.

COMPREHENSION RETEACH

Main Idea and Details

OBJECTIVE: *To identify a stated or an unstated main idea and recognize supporting details*

Focus

Share the following information with students:

> **The main idea is the most important thing a writer tries to tell readers. Writers give details to support, or tell more about, the main idea. Sometimes the writer tells readers what the main idea is; other times readers have to think about the other important details to figure it out.**

Choose a Teaching Model

VISUAL MODEL Introduce the model by telling students that there was a famous jazz musician named Louis Armstrong. Display or duplicate the following news story that might have appeared in a newspaper when Louis Armstrong was at the peak of his career.

> How do you become known as the first internationally famed soloist in jazz? Louis Armstrong has done it by being a great jazz trumpet player. At fourteen, he learned to play the cornet and then went on to play with some popular jazz bands. After making a series of records that rank among the greatest in jazz history, he traveled widely with a small group of musicians that he organized in the 1930s and 1940s. He has also appeared in many motion pictures.

Ask volunteers to tell in their own words what the main idea of the news story is. (Louis Armstrong was a famous, internationally known, jazz soloist.) Record the main idea on the board. Call on volunteers to write the details that support the main idea. Then follow the suggestions in **Summarize/Reinforce**.

AUDITORY MODEL Read aloud the news story used in the Visual Model. Ask students to state the main idea in their own words. (Louis Armstrong was a famous, internationally known, jazz soloist.) As you reread the story, stop and discuss each detail and ask whether it supports the main idea. Then follow the suggestions in **Summarize/Reinforce**.

KINESTHETIC/MOTOR MODEL Display the news story used in the Visual Model. Have students read the story silently and figure out the main idea. Then have them write the main idea in their own words. Ask students to work in small groups to agree on one main idea statement and act out the details that support the main idea. Have each group present the results in the form of a skit in which one student states the main idea and the others act out the details. Then follow the suggestions in **Summarize/Reinforce**.

Summarize/Reinforce

Have students summarize what they learned. (The main idea is the most important thing a writer wants to tell readers. Sometimes the main idea is stated. Other times, readers can figure out the main idea by thinking about the important details.) Reinforce the lesson by having students identify the main idea in an article from the sports page of your local paper. Remind students that paying attention to important details will help them figure out main ideas and better understand what they read.

A PLACE TO DREAM

Synthesizing Ideas

OBJECTIVE: *To combine the important parts of a story or an article in order to determine its overall, global meaning*

Focus

Share the following information with students:

A story contains many separate parts and ideas. *Synthesizing* means combining important ideas and parts to form one central idea. This helps readers to better understand what they read.

Choose a Teaching Model

VISUAL MODEL Have students reread the section titled "Conductor" on Student Anthology page 91, and identify the most important ideas. Write their suggestions on the board in the outer circles of a web similar to the following:

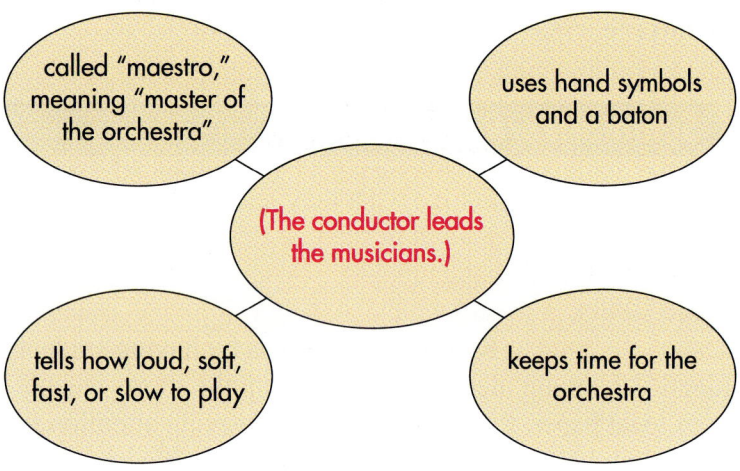

Then help students come up with a sentence that synthesizes the ideas, and write it in the oval in the center of the diagram. (A possible response is shown in parentheses.) Ask volunteers to reread each idea and to explain how it is related to the synthesis. Then follow the suggestions in **Summarize/Reinforce.**

AUDITORY MODEL Read aloud the section titled "Conductor" on Student Anthology page 91. Write on the board the statement that synthesizes the ideas in the center oval of the web in the Visual Model. Have students reread passage again to look for ideas that relate to the synthesizing statement. Ask volunteers to describe the related ideas. Write these ideas on the board in the form of a web similar to the one in the Visual Model. Ask volunteers to explain how each idea is related to the synthesis. Then follow the suggestions in **Summarize/Reinforce.**

KINESTHETIC/MOTOR MODEL Have students follow along as you read aloud the section titled "Conductor" on Student Anthology page 91. Help students come up with a sentence that summarizes this section. Write it on the board. (Accept reasonable responses: *The conductor leads the musicians.*) Then assign students to small groups and have each group choose an instrument from "Meet the Orchestra." Students will work together to list the details from their section on index cards, one idea per card. You may wish to have one student read each idea aloud as other students act it out. Then have the group write on a large piece of construction paper a statement that synthesizes all the ideas and arrange the details around it, similar to the web in the Visual Model. Finally, follow the suggestions in **Summarize/Reinforce.**

Summarize/Reinforce

Check students' understanding of the lesson by having them summarize what they learned. (By synthesizing, or combining the separate parts and ideas in a story to make one central idea, readers can better understand what they read.) You may want to reinforce the lesson by having students explain how the title "Meet the Orchestra" synthesizes all the ideas and parts of the selection. Remind students to use the information from the lesson to help them figure out the main point in the stories and articles they read.

STUDY SKILLS
RETEACH

Test-Taking

OBJECTIVE: *To develop and reinforce test-taking strategies*

Focus

Share with students the following information:

Three useful test-taking strategies are *scanning the entire test* **to find out what kind of questions have to be answered;** *developing a plan about what to do first and how much time to spend* **based on the kinds of questions there are and the amount of time there is to complete the test; and** *looking for clue words* **such as** *what* **and** *why* **to figure out what kind of information to include in each answer. Using these test-taking strategies helps students become more effective test takers.**

Choose a Teaching Model

VISUAL MODEL Write the test-taking strategies on the board. Provide students with unmarked copies of a test that includes sections with different types of questions (true-false, multiple-choice, fill-in). Read aloud each test-taking strategy, and ask students to apply it to the test. Have them use colored pencils or pens to write notes that indicate the kinds of questions on the test and circle the directions for each section and the clue words in each question. After students have finished, have them write a brief plan explaining how they would take the test if given thirty minutes. Have volunteers share their work. Then follow the suggestions in **Summarize/Reinforce**.

AUDITORY MODEL Ask students to take brief notes on each of the test-taking strategies that you mention. Then provide students with unmarked copies of a test similar to the one described in the Visual Model. Call on volunteers to respond orally to questions such as the following: "How many sections does this test have? What are the directions for each section? Where or how should you show your answers in this section? What clue words help you know the information to include in your answers? Which questions would you answer first? Why?" Then follow the suggestions in **Summarize/Reinforce**.

KINESTHETIC/MOTOR MODEL Provide students with unmarked copies of a test that includes sections with different types of test questions. Ask students to cut out the sections. Then have students perform the following tasks: circle the directions to each section, note the type of questions in each section and the way in which they should be answered, circle the clue words in each question, and note the information that should be included in the answer. Then have students arrange the sections to show in what order they would complete the sections. Ask volunteers to display and explain their work. Then follow the suggestions in **Summarize/Reinforce**.

Summarize/Reinforce

Check students' understanding of the lesson by having them summarize what they have learned. (Test-taking strategies include scanning the entire test, making a plan, and looking for clue words in each question.) You may want to reinforce the lesson by having students review these strategies before they take their next test. Remind students to use the strategies from this lesson to help them become more effective test takers.

GRAMMAR
RETEACH

Proper Nouns

OBJECTIVE: *To recognize and use proper nouns*

Focus

Share with students the following information:

> A *proper noun* names a particular person, place, or thing. All proper nouns begin with a capital letter. If a proper noun includes more than one word, the first letter of each important word is capitalized.

Choose a Teaching Model

VISUAL MODEL Display the following passage:

> Lydia plays saxophone in the Montgomery High School Jazz Band. Every Thanksgiving, the band gives a concert at the Alexander Center for the Study of Music. The center is located in the town of Somers. Everybody's favorite song is "Take the A Train," by Duke Ellington. Mr. Sims, the bandleader, makes sure the band plays this song each year.

Ask volunteers to underline the proper nouns in the passage. Then display the following chart:

Particular Person, Place, or Thing	Proper Noun
name of saxophone player	(Lydia)
name of band	(Montgomery High School Jazz Band)
name of holiday	(Thanksgiving)
name of music school	(Alexander Center for the Study of Music)
song title	("Take the A Train")
name of composer	(Duke Ellington)
name of bandleader	(Mr. Sims)

Ask students to copy the chart and to write the proper nouns from the passage in the appropriate boxes in the chart. Next, have volunteers share their answers by writing them on the chart on the board. Discuss the capitalization of the proper nouns, particularly that of the important words in "Alexander Center for the Study of Music" and "Take the A Train." Then follow the suggestions in **Summarize/Reinforce**.

AUDITORY MODEL Display the passage and the chart from the Visual Model. Ask volunteers to name the proper nouns in the passage. Underline them as they are identified. Have students copy the chart. Next, point to each proper noun, and ask students which particular person, place, or thing it names. Have students record the answers in their chart. Ask volunteers to share their answers by reading aloud the names on their charts. Discuss the capitalization of the important words in "Alexander Center for the Study of Music" and "Take the A Train." Then follow the suggestions in **Summarize/Reinforce**.

KINESTHETIC/MOTOR MODEL Distribute copies of the passage from the Visual Model, and have students underline the proper nouns. Next, have students work in pairs to cut out the proper nouns and paste them onto a chart with the same categories as on the Visual Model. Have pairs exchange their charts and check each other's work. Ask volunteers to transfer their answers to the board. Finally, discuss the capitalization of the important words in "Take the A Train" and "Alexander Center for the Study of Music." Then follow the suggestions in **Summarize/Reinforce**.

Summarize/Reinforce

Check understanding of the lesson by having students summarize what they have learned. (A proper noun names a particular person, place, or thing and begins with a capital letter. When a proper noun includes more than one word, the important words are capitalized.) You may want to reinforce the lesson by having students look for proper nouns in a recent reading assignment. Remind students that the information in this lesson can help them use proper nouns correctly in their writing.

Structural Clues

OBJECTIVE: *To use structural analysis for independent decoding of words*

Focus

Share the following information with students:

Readers can often figure out the meaning and pronunciation of an unfamiliar word by studying the word's parts, including the base word, prefix, and/or suffix. Prefixes change the meanings of the words, and suffixes change the meanings and how the words are used. Using structural clues can help readers figure out many unfamiliar words.

Choose a Teaching Model

VISUAL MODEL Write on the board the following affixes and their meanings:

un- = "not"

-ful = "full of"

Then display the following paragraph on the board:

> The crowd waiting on the lawn was <u>unhappy</u>. The band's <u>wonderful</u> performance had come to a sudden halt. A strong wind had blown away the musicians' sheet music! Instead of giving up, the musicians played from memory.

Have students read the paragraph silently and copy the underlined words. Tell them to circle the base words in *unhappy* and *wonderful*. Then have students look at the two affixes and their meanings listed on the board and figure out which affix appears in each word. Have students use these structural clues as well as sentence context to match each word to one of these meanings: "not happy," and "full of wonder." Call on volunteers to tell how they figured out the meanings. Then follow the suggestions in **Summarize/Reinforce**.

AUDITORY MODEL Write on the board the affixes and their meanings from the Visual Model. Organize students into pairs, and assign one affix to each student. Read aloud the passage from the Visual Model. Have students listen for the word that contains their particular affix. Reread the paragraph slowly, and have students raise their hands when they hear the word containing their affix. List on the board and say the words *unhappy* and *wonderful*. Next, distribute a copy of the paragraph to each group, and have students work together to figure out the meanings of the underlined words. Have them say the correct meaning for each word: "not happy" and "full of wonder." Have volunteers share what they figured out. Then follow the suggestions in **Summarize/Reinforce**.

KINESTHETIC/MOTOR MODEL Display the paragraph from the Visual Model. Read the paragraph aloud. Then write these meanings on the board: "not happy,"; "full of wonder." Have each student copy the two underlined words, circle the base word in each, and next to it write the appropriate meaning. Encourage students to tell how they arrived at those meanings. Then follow the suggestions in **Summarize/Reinforce**.

Summarize/Reinforce

Check students' understanding of the lesson by having them summarize what they learned. (Readers can often use what they know about word parts to figure out the meanings of unfamiliar words. They can also use context clues to figure out the pronunciations and meanings of these words.) You may want to reinforce the lesson by writing new words that contain affixes from the lesson and by having students create oral context sentences for these words. Remind students that using structural clues can help readers better understand what they read.

GRAMMAR
RETEACH

Singular and Plural Nouns

OBJECTIVE: *To recognize and use singular and plural nouns*

Focus

Share the following with students:

> A *singular noun* names one person, place, or thing. A *plural noun* names more than one person, place, or thing. Most plural nouns are formed by adding *-s* or *-es* to the end of singular nouns. Knowing how to recognize and form singular and plural nouns helps readers understand what they read and become better writers.

Choose a Teaching Model

VISUAL MODEL Write the following paragraph on the board:

> The <u>cartoon</u> on <u>television</u> was unusual. A <u>fox</u> dropped some <u>crackers</u> onto the <u>bushes</u>. They turned into <u>airplanes</u>. The <u>girl</u> threw two <u>apples</u> into the <u>clouds</u>. They turned into <u>balloons</u>.

Have students read the passage silently. Then suggest that pairs of students make a list of the singular nouns and the plural nouns. Ask volunteers to come to the board and to write their answers in a chart like the one below.

Singular	Plural
cartoon	
television	
fox	
	crackers
	bushes
	airplanes
girl	
	apples
	clouds
	balloons

Have volunteers write the corresponding singular or plural form of each noun in the chart. Circle the ending of each plural noun, and point out that all the plural nouns end in *-s* or *-es*. Then follow the suggestions in **Summarize/Reinforce**.

AUDITORY MODEL Have students name an object or objects that they see on the way to school. List these nouns on the board. Then have students tell whether each noun is singular or plural. Record the responses on the board in a chart similar to the one in the Visual Model. Then have pairs of students name and write the corresponding singular or plural form of each noun in the chart. Also tell students to say the endings of the plural nouns. Have volunteers add their answers to the chart on the board. Discuss the endings of the plural nouns. Then follow the suggestions in **Summarize/Reinforce**.

KINESTHETIC/MOTOR MODEL On individual word cards, write one singular or plural noun. (suggestions: *tree, playground, friend, bushes, television, fox, airplanes, lunches, clouds, telephone poles, apples*) Create one card for each student, and place the slips upside down in a pile. Write the words *Singular* and *Plural* on the board as column heads. Have students take turns picking a card, reading the noun aloud, and telling whether the noun is singular or plural. Have students tape their cards under the appropriate column heads. Then have students work in pairs to write the singular form of each plural noun and the plural form of each singular noun. Follow the suggestions in **Summarize/Reinforce**.

Summarize/Reinforce

Check students' understanding of the lesson by having them summarize what they learned. (Singular nouns name one person, place, or thing. Plural nouns name more than one. Most plural nouns are formed by adding an *-s* or *-es* to the end of singular nouns.) You may want to reinforce the lesson by having students generate their own lists of singular and plural nouns. Remind students that the information in this lesson will help them use singular and plural nouns correctly when they write.

DECODING
RETEACH

Structural Analysis

OBJECTIVE: *To use prefixes, base words, and suffixes to decode words*

Focus

Share the following information with students:

> **Readers can use what they know about prefixes and suffixes to help them determine the pronunciations and meanings of unfamiliar words. A *prefix* is a word part that comes at the beginning of a word and changes the meaning of the base word. A *suffix* is a word part that comes at the end of the word and changes the meaning of the base word and the way it is used.**

Choose a Teaching Model

VISUAL MODEL Write the following affixes and their meanings on the board:

re-	"again"	*-less*	"without"
un-	"not"	*-ly*	"in a way that is"
-ful	"full of"		

Then display or duplicate the following pairs of sentences without underlining any words:

1. Many people fear that bats might <u>harm</u> them. In fact, bats are <u>harmless</u> and can be <u>good</u> neighbors because they eat mosquitoes.
2. The thunder was very loud and quite <u>sudden</u>. We had never seen a storm begin so <u>suddenly</u>.
3. I like to <u>write</u> stories. Sometimes I decide to <u>rewrite</u> them to make them even better.
4. Some snacks, like fruit, add to our <u>health</u>. These <u>healthful</u> snacks can be very tasty.
5. <u>Unripe</u> tomatoes are green. Buy only the <u>ripe</u> red ones, please.

Ask students to read each pair of sentences silently. Have volunteers identify in each pair the word that is the base word and the word with a prefix or suffix. Write the word with the affix on the board. Then have the volunteers circle each base word and discuss how the meaning or usage of that base word is affected by the addition of the prefix or suffix. Then follow the suggestions in **Summarize/Reinforce.**

AUDITORY MODEL Say and write on the board the affixes and their meanings from the Visual Model. Then read aloud the pairs of sentences in that model. Ask students to listen carefully and identify the word that sounds similar to another word in the sentence pair except that it has a prefix or suffix. Next, say and write on the board the word with the affix and the word without the affix. For the word with the affix, have volunteers tell which part is the base word and which part is the prefix or suffix. Then have them explain how the affix changes the meaning of the base word. Encourage students to use context clues. Then follow the suggestions in **Summarize/Reinforce.**

KINESTHETIC/MOTOR MODEL Assign students to groups of four. Distribute ten index cards to each group and tell students to write each of the affixes listed in the Visual Model on the front of an index card and its meaning on the back. Then have students write these base words on the other cards: *harm, sudden, write, health,* and *ripe.* Ask students to divide up the affix cards and base word cards so that each group member has one of each. Read aloud each pair of sentences listed in the Visual Model and ask students to listen for the affixes and words shown on their cards. Students should then work together to use the cards to build the word with the prefix or suffix. Have group members discuss the difference between the meaning or usage of the base word and the meaning of the word when the affix is added. Then follow the suggestions in **Summarize/Reinforce.**

Summarize/Reinforce

Have students summarize what they have learned. (Prefixes and suffixes are word parts that, when added to a base word, change the meaning of that word. Suffixes can change the way in which a word is used.) To reinforce the lesson, have students work in pairs to list other words that include the affixes from this lesson. Remind students to use what they have learned in this lesson when they come across unfamiliar words in their reading.

COMPREHENSION
RETEACH

Author's Purpose

OBJECTIVE: *To identify an author's main purpose for writing*

Focus

Share the following information with students:

An *author's purpose* may be to inform, to entertain, or to provide directions. Readers can often figure out an author's purpose by previewing what they read. Nonfiction selections may include subheads, photographs, or illustrations. Readers should read nonfiction selections more slowly than fiction stories in order to understand new facts and vocabulary. Knowing how to identify an author's purpose helps readers better understand and enjoy what they read.

Choose a Teaching Model

VISUAL MODEL Gather a group of books that entertain, inform, or provide directions. One by one, hold up books for students to see. Ask volunteers to come up and read the titles, describe the covers, and describe the information on some of the inside pages. Have students decide whether the author's purpose is to inform, to entertain, or to provide directions. Then display the chart below, and enter each title and author in the appropriate column.

To Inform	To Entertain	To Provide Directions

Discuss with volunteers how they identified the author's purpose for each book on the chart. Then follow the suggestions in **Summarize/Reinforce**.

AUDITORY MODEL Have each student choose three books, magazine articles, or anthology selections they have read. One should be fiction, one should be nonfiction, and one should provide directions. Next, have students pair off and discuss the books or articles they have selected. Partners should decide the author's purpose for each selection. Then have students role-play the authors of the books or articles, and give a short speech to their classmates about why they wrote each one. Prompt them to begin with, "Hello, I'm [author's name], and I wrote [book title] because. . . ." Also have students explain whether the books contain facts, stories, or directions. Then follow the suggestions in **Summarize/Reinforce**.

KINESTHETIC/MOTOR MODEL Gather a group of books that inform, entertain, or provide directions. Write these headings on the board: *To Inform, To Entertain,* and *To Provide Directions*. Assign students to groups of four, and give each group a stack of books. Have group members look through each book and identify the author's purpose. Then have members take turns writing each title and author under the appropriate heading on the board. Continue until all the books have been classified. Ask volunteers to discuss their answers and explain whether the books contain facts, stories, or directions. Then follow the suggestions in **Summarize/Reinforce**.

Summarize/Reinforce

Check students' understanding of the lesson by having them summarize what they learned. (An author's purpose for writing may be to entertain, to give information, or to explain how to do something.) You may want to reinforce the lesson by having students identify the author's purpose for a story or an article they have read recently. Remind students to use the information from the lesson to help them better understand and enjoy what they read.

GRAMMAR RETEACH

More Plural Nouns

OBJECTIVE: *To correctly form plural nouns and irregular plural nouns*

Focus

Share the following information with students:

Not all *plural nouns* are formed in the same way. For nouns that end in a consonant + *y*, the plural is formed by changing the *y* to an *i* and adding *es*, as in *lady/ladies* and *party/parties*. Some nouns have a plural form that does not follow a regular pattern. Knowing how to form plural nouns will help students when they read and write.

Choose a Teaching Model

VISUAL MODEL Display and distribute the paragraph below:

Dr. Hall was a special <u>woman</u>. When <u>children</u> went to her to have their <u>teeth</u> cleaned, she asked about their <u>hobbies</u>. One <u>child</u> helped his parents raise <u>puppies</u>. Another collected postcards of his <u>city</u>. Another drew cartoons of <u>mice</u>. One child hiked with his parents. Were his <u>feet</u> sore!

On the board, list each underlined noun. Have students read the paragraph silently, copy the list of nouns, and write next to it the corresponding singular or plural noun. Then follow the suggestions in **Summarize/Reinforce**.

AUDITORY MODEL Display the paragraph from the Visual Model, and read it aloud. Then read aloud each underlined noun. Ask students to name the equivalent singular or plural noun. Have each student say and list the pairs of nouns on a sheet of paper. Guide students in writing. Then ask volunteers to read each singular-plural noun pair aloud. Finally, follow the suggestions in **Summarize/ Reinforce**.

KINESTHETIC/MOTOR MODEL Display the paragraph from the Visual Model, and list on the board each underlined noun. Have students make word cards for each underlined noun and its equivalent singular or plural form. Then encourage students to take turns picking up a card, stating whether the noun is singular or plural, and using the noun in a sentence. Have them hold up the index card at the point that they say the noun. Then follow the suggestions in **Summarize/Reinforce**.

Summarize/Reinforce

Check students' understanding of the lesson by having them summarize what they learned. (Some singular nouns change spelling in the plural form. When a singular noun ends in a consonant + *y*, the *y* is changed to *i*, and *es* is added. Some plural noun forms are irregular.) You may wish to reinforce the lesson by having students scan newspaper headlines for plural nouns. Remind students that knowing how to form plural nouns helps readers understand what they read and become better writers.

A PLACE TO DREAM

Point of View

OBJECTIVE: *To determine whether a story is told from the first- or third-person point of view*

Focus

Share the following information with students:

> The *point of view* of a story is the way in which an author chooses to see and tell a story. Stories told from the *first-person point of view* are told by a character in the story. This character refers to himself or herself as *I*. Stories told from the *third-person point of view* are told by an outside observer. In a story told in the third person, all the characters are referred to as *he* or *she*. Knowing the point of view of a story helps readers better understand what they read.

Choose a Teaching Model

VISUAL MODEL Display the following sentences, and have students copy them:

- **Renée put on her boots before she went outside.**
- **Ramon did not go outside because he had a cold.**
- **I wanted to take my dog Sparky to the park.**
- **Sparky came running when I called him.**

Tell students to identify and label the point of view of each sentence and circle the words in each sentence that helped them figure out the point of view. Ask volunteers to share their answers with their classmates. Then have students rewrite the sentences in the alternate point of view, and switch sentences with a partner to check each other's work. Finally, ask volunteers to read their sentences aloud. Then follow the suggestions in **Summarize/Reinforce**.

AUDITORY MODEL Model for students how to turn a comic strip into a first-person or a third-person story. Choose a character and say, "I am going to be [character's name], and I am going to tell from the first-person point of view what happens in this comic strip." Then relate the events in the comic strip in the first-person. Next, tell the comic strip story from the third-person point of view. Hand out two comic strips to each pair of students, and have partners repeat the procedure you modeled. To assess students' understanding, ask volunteers to narrate their strips for their classmates, using a first- or third-person point of view. Also have volunteers explain whether the narrator is a story character or an outside observer. Then follow the suggestions in **Summarize/Reinforce**.

KINESTHETIC/MOTOR MODEL Distribute one comic strip to each pair of students. Have partners paste the comic strip in the center of a large piece of paper. Above the strip, have one partner rewrite the comic strip from the point of view of one of the story characters, using a first-person point of view. Below the strip, have the other partner rewrite what happens from the third-person point of view. You may wish to model this process by displaying a comic strip on the board and writing a first- and third-person narration. Ask volunteers to read their comic strip stories to their classmates. Then follow the suggestions in **Summarize/Reinforce**.

Summarize/Reinforce

Check students' understanding of the lesson by having them summarize what they learned. (*A story with a first-person point of view is told by a story character who refers to himself or herself as I. A story with a third-person point of view is told by an outside narrator who refers to story characters as he or she.*) You may want to reinforce the lesson by having students identify the point of view of stories they have read recently. Remind students to use the information from this lesson to help them enjoy and understand the stories they read.

GRAMMAR
RETEACH

Singular Possessive Nouns

OBJECTIVE: *To recognize and understand singular possessive nouns*

Focus

Share the following with students:

A *singular possessive noun* shows ownership by one person or thing. To form a singular possessive noun, add an apostrophe + *s* to the end of a singular noun. Knowing how singular possessive nouns are formed helps students when they read and write.

Choose a Teaching Model

VISUAL MODEL Display the following sentences:

- **My father's house is full of visitors.**
- **The candle's light warmed the room.**
- **My sister's coat is green.**
- **We decorated the dog's collar with a bow.**

Have students copy the sentences. When they have finished, read each sentence aloud as students follow along silently. Tell students to underline the word in each sentence that is possessive and to circle the part of the noun that shows this ownership. Model this process by underlining *father's* in the first sentence and circling the apostrophe and *s*. Ask volunteers to transfer their answers to the sentences on the board. Then have pairs of students write four sentences that contain singular possessive nouns. Suggest to partners that they write about things that belong to each other. Ask volunteers to write their sentences on the board. Go over the structure of each possessive noun. Then follow the suggestions in **Summarize/Reinforce**.

AUDITORY MODEL Display the sentences from the Visual Model. Read the first sentence aloud, and ask students "Whose house is it?" *(My father's)* Then circle the part of the noun that shows it is possessive. Repeat this process for each of the remaining sentences. Next, have students work in groups of six. Assign each group member a different number between 1 and 6. Give each group a six-sided cube, and have students sit in a circle. Have a member roll the cube and make up a sentence about the group member whose number corresponds to the number on the cube. (Example: *Tina's shoes are red.*) Then have that member take a turn. Remind students to use possessive nouns in their sentences. Observe the groups as they perform the activity. Help members who are having difficulty. Finally, ask six volunteers to play a few rounds of the game for the other students. Write down the sentences students create, and underline the apostrophe + *s* at the end of each possessive noun. Then follow the suggestions in **Summarize/Reinforce**.

KINESTHETIC/MOTOR MODEL Display the sentences from the Visual Model, and give each student a copy of the sentences. Have pairs of students illustrate two of the sentences from the list, cut out the singular possessive nouns from the sentences they illustrated, and paste them under the pictures. Ask volunteers to share their work by displaying their pictures and writing the possessive nouns on the board. Have them circle the apostrophe + *s* in each noun. Then follow the suggestions in **Summarize/Reinforce**.

Summarize/Reinforce

Check students' understanding of the lesson by having them summarize what they learned. *(Singular possessive nouns show ownership by one person or thing. To form a singular possessive noun, add an apostrophe + s to the end of a singular noun.)* You may want to reinforce the lesson by having students find singular possessive nouns in another story they recently read. Remind students to use the information in this lesson to help them use singular possessive nouns correctly when they write.

LITERARY APPRECIATION
RETEACH

Story Elements

OBJECTIVE: *To use details to gain information about setting, characters, and plot*

Focus

Share with students the following information:

The questions "Who?" "When?" "Where?" and "What happened?" help you identify the story elements of *characters, setting, problem, important events,* and *solution.*

Choose a Teaching Model

VISUAL MODEL Display the following paragraph:

> On Monday afternoon Carla visited Mrs. San Carlos. Mrs. San Carlos lived in an apartment building across the street. She was not feeling well, so Carla took her some warm soup. Mrs. San Carlos was too sick to drive, so Carla went to the market for her.

Ask students to read the paragraph silently and to underline details that tell *who,* circle details that tell *where* and *when,* and draw boxes around details that tell *what* happens. Then display the following diagram and have students copy it:

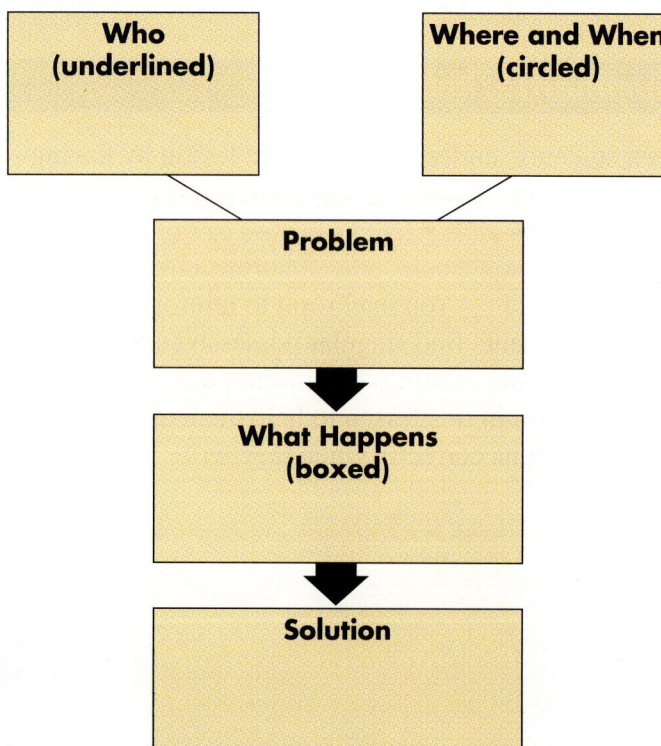

Have students follow the directions in parentheses to help them fill in the diagram. Then follow the suggestions in **Summarize/Reinforce.**

AUDITORY MODEL Distribute copies of the paragraph from the Visual Model to pairs of students. Read the paragraph aloud as students follow along silently. Next, ask partners to tell each other the details that tell *who* the story is about, that tell *when* and *where* the story takes place, and that tell *what* happens. Ask volunteers to share their answers. Next, pose the following questions, and ask volunteers to answer them: "Who are the characters in this story? What is the story's setting? What is the plot?" Then follow the suggestions in **Summarize/Reinforce.**

KINESTHETIC/MOTOR MODEL Display and distribute the paragraph from the Visual Model. Have students discuss *who* the story is about, *where* and *when* it happens, and *what* happens. Next, have students work in pairs to create and label a poster of a story map. Have students display their posters in the classroom. Then follow the suggestions in **Summarize/Reinforce.**

Summarize/Reinforce

Check students' understanding of the lesson by having them summarize what they have learned. (Asking *who, when, where,* and *what happened* helps readers understand the characters, setting, problem, important events, and solution.) You may want to reinforce the lesson by having students use story details to gather information about the characters, setting, and plot of another story they have read. Remind students to use the information from this lesson to help them better understand what they read.

GRAMMAR
RETEACH

Plural Possessive Nouns

OBJECTIVE: *To recognize and form plural possessive nouns*

Focus

Share with students the following information:

> A *plural possessive noun* shows ownership by more than one person or thing. To form the possessive of a plural noun that ends in *s*, add an apostrophe to the end of the word. Knowing how to recognize and form plural possessive nouns helps students become better readers and writers.

Choose a Teaching Model

VISUAL MODEL Display the following passage, omitting the underlining:

> My <u>grandparents'</u> farm is in Oklahoma. The <u>horses</u> are kept in a barn. The <u>cows'</u> mooing is loudest at feeding time. The <u>chickens</u> live in a small house called a coop. The <u>pigs'</u> pen is filled with mud. My <u>cousins</u> help take care of the farm.

Ask a volunteer to underline all the plural possessive nouns in the passage. Then ask another volunteer to circle all the plural nouns that are not possessive. Have students copy the six words into a chart like the following one:

Plural Nouns	Plural Possessive Nouns

Then have students work in pairs to make the plural nouns possessive. Have them record their answers in the second column of their charts. Ask volunteers to share their answers by writing them on the board. Ask students to tell what letter they looked for before they added the apostrophe to each plural noun. Then follow the suggestions in **Summarize/Reinforce**.

AUDITORY MODEL Display and read aloud the passage from the Visual Model, omitting the underlining. Point to and say the plural nouns and plural possessive nouns one at a time, and ask whether the noun shows ownership. Record students' responses on the board in a chart like the one in the Visual Model. Discuss with students what they would have to do to make each plural noun possessive. Have volunteers write the answers on the board. Then follow the suggestions in **Summarize/Reinforce**.

KINESTHETIC/MOTOR MODEL Create a set of plural-noun cards. Make at least one card for each student. Write a plural noun or a plural possessive noun on each card. Next, display the passage from the Visual Model, omitting the underlining, and help students identify the plural nouns and the plural possessive nouns in the passage. Make the plural nouns possessive, and discuss how this is done. Then ask students to come to the front of the room, choose a card, and tell whether the noun on the card shows ownership. If it does not, have the student write the possessive form of the word in the chart on the board. Then follow the suggestions in **Summarize/Reinforce**.

Summarize/Reinforce

Check understanding of the lesson by having students summarize what they have learned. (To make a plural noun that ends in *s* show ownership, add an apostrophe to the end.) You may want to reinforce the lesson by having students look for plural possessive nouns in other stories they read. Remind students to use the information from this lesson to help them become better readers and writers.

LITERARY APPRECIATION
RETEACH

Figurative Language

OBJECTIVE: *To appreciate idioms, similes, and metaphors*

Focus

Share with students the following information:

> Authors use *figurative language* to create vivid pictures. An *idiom* is an expression that has a meaning different from the meaning of the words in it. For example, *I could eat a horse* means "I am very hungry." A *simile* compares two unlike things using the word *like* or *as.* For example, *I'm as hungry as a bear.* A *metaphor* makes a comparison by saying one thing *is* another thing. For example, *My hunger is a roaring tiger inside me.* Recognizing figurative language helps readers understand what they read.

Choose a Teaching Model

VISUAL MODEL Display the following sentences, omitting the underlining and the words in parentheses:

- The fish scales were shiny as silver. (simile)
- "Time to turn in for the night," said Grandpa. (idiom)
- The knife was a flash of light in Grandpa's quick hands. (metaphor)
- They broke camp in the morning. (idiom)
- Justin's bed was as neat as a pin. (simile)
- The trail was a thread between the rocks. (metaphor)

Have students read the sentences silently. Point to the first sentence, and underline the simile. Ask students to tell what two things are being compared. (fish scales and silver) Circle the word *as,* and write the word *simile* next to the sentence. Follow the same procedure for the second sentence (an idiom) and the third sentence (a metaphor). Then have students copy the three remaining sentences, underline the figurative phrase in each, and label it *simile, idiom,* or *metaphor.* Ask volunteers to share their answers. Then follow the suggestions in **Summarize/Reinforce.**

AUDITORY MODEL Display the list of sentences from the Visual Model, omitting the underlining and the words in parentheses. Distribute copies of the list to students. Read the sentences aloud as students follow along silently. Next, ask each of the following questions aloud: "Which two sentences make a comparison using *like* or *as*? Which two sentences make a comparison by saying that one thing is another thing? Which two sentences contain an idiom?" Have volunteers answer by reading aloud the figurative phrases while other students underline the phrases on their copies of the sentences. Transfer the underlining to the sentences on the board. Ask volunteers to explain the meanings of the expressions. Then follow the suggestions in **Summarize/Reinforce.**

KINESTHETIC/MOTOR MODEL Display the sentences from the Visual Model, omitting the underlining and the words in parentheses, along with the following chart:

Idiom	Simile	Metaphor

Have students work in pairs to copy the sentences and the chart. Model identifying the simile, idiom, and metaphor in the first three sentences. Then have partners identify which type of figurative language is in each of the other three sentences. Ask partners to cut out each sentence and to paste it into the correct column in the chart. Have volunteers discuss their answers. Finally, discuss the meaning of each figurative expression. Then follow the suggestions in **Summarize/Reinforce.**

Summarize/Reinforce

Check understanding of the lesson by having students summarize what they have learned. (Authors use figurative language to make their writing livelier. Idioms, similes, and metaphors are examples of figurative language.) You may want to reinforce the lesson by having students make lists of the similes, metaphors, and idioms that they find in the stories they read. Have students illustrate and publish their lists. Remind students to use the information from this lesson to help them understand what they read.

GRAMMAR RETEACH

Singular and Plural Pronouns

OBJECTIVE: *To recognize and correctly use singular and plural pronouns*

Focus

Share the following information with students:

> A *pronoun* is a word that takes the place of one or more nouns. The *singular pronouns I, me, you, she, he, him, her,* and *it* replace singular nouns. *I* is always capitalized. The *plural pronouns we, you, they, us,* and *them* replace plural nouns. Being able to recognize singular and plural pronouns helps readers better understand what they read and helps writers create more interesting stories.

Choose a Teaching Model

VISUAL MODEL Display the following paragraph:

> Little Gopher couldn't find his brushes. <u>He</u> looked for <u>them</u> everywhere. <u>He</u> even looked on the hill, but <u>they</u> weren't there. So Little Gopher asked the Indian maiden for help. <u>She</u> told <u>him</u> to look under the rocks. But <u>they</u> were too heavy to lift alone. "Please help <u>me</u>," Little Gopher said to his mother. Together <u>they</u> lifted the rocks and found the brushes.

Read the paragraph aloud. Then have students write the headings *Singular Pronouns* and *Plural Pronouns* on a sheet of paper and list each underlined pronoun from the paragraph under the correct column head. Next to each pronoun in the chart, have students list the noun or nouns it replaces. Have volunteers read aloud the sentences from the paragraph, tell whether each underlined pronoun is singular or plural, and identify the noun or nouns replaced by each pronoun. Next, have students write a paragraph of their own about something that might happen to Little Gopher. Ask them to use at least two pronouns in their paragraphs. Have volunteers read their paragraphs aloud, identify the pronouns, and then identify the nouns they replace. Then follow the suggestions in **Summarize/Reinforce**.

AUDITORY MODEL Read aloud the singular and plural pronouns as you write them in two lists on the board. Display the paragraph from the Visual Model, omitting the underlining. Read the paragraph aloud, and have students listen for pronouns. Read the paragraph a second time, and have students raise their hands when they hear a pronoun. Have volunteers orally identify the noun or nouns each pronoun replaces. Then ask students to write four sentences about Little Gopher. Tell them to use at least two pronouns in their sentences. Have volunteers read their sentences aloud, identify the pronouns, and tell which noun or nouns each one replaces. Then follow the suggestions in **Summarize/Reinforce**.

KINESTHETIC/MOTOR MODEL Write the singular and plural pronouns in two lists on the board. Rewrite the paragraph from the Visual Model on the board so that each underlined pronoun is replaced by the noun or nouns it refers to (*He*—Little Gopher; *them*—the brushes; *He*—Little Gopher; *it*—the hill; *She*—the Indian maiden; *him*—Little Gopher; *they*—the rocks; *me*—Little Gopher; *they*—Little Gopher and his mother). Underline those nouns. Read the paragraph aloud. Have volunteers come to the board, read aloud a sentence, erase the underlined noun(s), and replace it (them) with the appropriate pronoun(s). Have volunteers read the new sentence aloud. Then follow the suggestions in **Summarize/Reinforce**.

Summarize/Reinforce

Check students' understanding of the lesson by having them summarize what they learned. (A pronoun is a word that replaces one or more nouns. *I, me, you, he, she, him, her,* and *it* are singular pronouns. *We, you, they, us,* and *them* are plural pronouns.) To reinforce the lesson, duplicate a passage from a story students have read recently, and have them circle all the pronouns and then identify the noun or nouns each one replaces. Remind students that being able to recognize and use singular and plural pronouns will make them better readers and writers.

COMPREHENSION
RETEACH

Making Predictions

OBJECTIVE: *To use text and personal experience to predict story events*

Focus

Share the following information with students:

> Readers can use story information along with their own knowledge to predict what is going to happen in a story. Being able to make predictions helps readers become more involved in what they read.

Choose a Teaching Model

VISUAL MODEL Display or duplicate the following passage:

> All day long Tanya had been waiting to go to her grandparents' apartment. It was her birthday. She knew they would have a present for her. As she and her mother reached the top of the stairs, she saw that her grandparents' door was open. But as she walked in, she heard a surprising noise coming from the kitchen. It sounded like barking, but she knew that her grandparents did not have a dog. Then she noticed a bowl of water on the floor.

Have students read the passage. Then draw the following diagram on the board:

Story Clues + What I Know = Prediction

Discuss with students how they might fill in the diagram, using story clues and personal knowledge to make a prediction. Then follow the suggestions in **Summarize/ Reinforce.**

AUDITORY MODEL Read aloud the passage from the Visual Model. Stop at various points to ask, "What do you know so far? What do you think will happen next? How do you know?" Then follow the suggestions in **Summarize/ Reinforce.**

KINESTHETIC/MOTOR MODEL Display or read aloud the passage from the Visual Model. Invite students to work together to draw a series of cartoons showing the events of the story in sequence. Then have students draw what they think will happen next. Ask volunteers to show their cartoons to classmates and explain what story information and personal knowledge helped them make their predictions. Then follow the suggestions in **Summarize/Reinforce.**

Summarize/Reinforce

Have students summarize what they learned. (To predict what will happen next in a story, use story information and personal experience.) To reinforce the lesson, frequently ask students to tell what predictions they made while reading selections and to explain what led them to make those predictions. Remind them to use the strategies from this lesson to help them make predictions as they read.

GRAMMAR
RETEACH

Subject Pronouns

OBJECTIVE: *To recognize and use subject pronouns*

Focus

Share the following information with students:

> A *subject pronoun* is a word that takes the place of one or more nouns in the subject of a sentence. The words *I, you, he, she, it, we,* and *they* are subject pronouns. Knowing how to recognize and use subject pronouns helps students become better readers and writers.

Choose a Teaching Model

VISUAL MODEL List the subject pronouns on the board. Then display the following paragraph about the story "Paddington Paints a Picture," omitting the underlining:

> <u>I</u> think Paddington always gets into trouble. <u>He</u> saw Mr. Gruber clean a painting. <u>It</u> had a masterpiece underneath. Paddington tried to do the same with Mr. Brown's painting but made a mess instead. Then Miss Black came to the Browns' house. <u>She</u> took the painting to the judges. <u>They</u> liked the painting and gave Mr. Brown the first prize. Can <u>you</u> believe that silly bear?

Read the paragraph aloud. Have a volunteer underline each subject pronoun. Ask students to make a list of the subject pronouns and the noun or nouns each one replaces. Have volunteers share their answers. (If necessary, explain that *you* refers to one individual or to a whole group.) Then follow the suggestions in **Summarize/Reinforce**.

AUDITORY MODEL Display a list of the subject pronouns *I, you, he, she, it, we,* and *they.* Write on the board the name of each character from "Paddington Paints a Picture": Mr. Brown, Paddington, Mr. Gruber, Mrs. Bird, Miss Black, Mrs. Brown, Jonathan, Judy, Man. Circle one or two of the names, and have a student orally compose a sentence about the character(s), using the name(s) as the subject(s) of the sentence. Repeat the sentence as you write it on the board, underlining the subject(s). Then call on another volunteer to orally compose another sentence about the same character(s), using a subject pronoun to replace or refer to the original subject(s). Repeat this process until each student has had a chance to compose a sentence. Next, have students compose sentences about each other or themselves, using the subject pronouns *I* and *you.* Then follow the suggestions in **Summarize/Reinforce**.

KINESTHETIC/MOTOR MODEL Provide each student with eight index cards. Have students write each subject pronoun on a separate card, and make two cards for "you." Then write on the board the character names from the Auditory Model. Have students write two sentences with singular subjects and a third sentence with a plural subject. (For example: Mr. Brown and Mrs. Brown liked Paddington.) Then have students take turns writing one of their sentences on the board, reading it aloud, and underlining the subject(s). Ask the other students to figure out which subject pronoun could replace the subject(s) and to hold up the appropriate index card. Call on a volunteer to orally revise the original sentence by using a subject pronoun. Repeat the procedure several times. Next, group students in pairs. Have each student write a sentence using his or her own name and one sentence using his or her partner's name as the subject. Ask partners to read their sentences to each other, replacing each subject with the appropriate subject pronoun, either *I* or *you.* Then follow the suggestions in **Summarize/Reinforce**.

Summarize/Reinforce

Check students' understanding of the lesson by having them summarize what they learned. (Subject pronouns take the place of the noun or nouns in the subject of a sentence. *I, you, he, she, it, we,* and *they* are subject pronouns.) To reinforce this lesson, have students make a list of the subject pronouns in a passage from a story they have read recently, and have them identify the subjects that those pronouns replace. Remind students that being able to recognize and use subject pronouns helps readers understand what they read and helps writers write more interesting stories.

VOCABULARY RETEACH

Context Clues

OBJECTIVE: *To use context clues to determine word meanings*

Focus

Share the following information with students:

Readers may come across unfamiliar words as they read. To figure out the meanings of these words, readers may look for clues in the surrounding text. This is called using *context clues*.

Choose a Teaching Model

VISUAL MODEL Write the following sentence on the board:

> At first Paddington was <u>confident</u> about finding an old master's painting under Mr. Brown's painting, but soon he began to feel less sure of himself.

Read the sentence aloud, pointing out the underlined word. Then circle the context clues (*but, feel less sure of himself*) and explain how they help the reader figure out the meaning of the underlined word. Next, display or duplicate the following sentences and definitions:

1. Mr. Gruber paid close attention to his painting, but Paddington was <u>distracted</u>.
2. The man showed that the painting was <u>edible</u> by eating a marmalade chunk.
3. Mrs. Bird was very <u>agitated</u> about Mr. Brown's painting, and Paddington was upset, too.

    __(2)__ "good for eating"

    __(1)__ "not paying attention"

    __(3)__ "worried"

Have students read the sentences silently and think about the meaning of each underlined word. Then have volunteers read each sentence aloud and write the sentence number in the blank next to the correct definition. Ask volunteers to circle the context clues they used to figure out their answers. Then follow the suggestions in **Summarize/Reinforce.**

AUDITORY MODEL Read aloud the example sentence from the Visual Model. Model how to use context clues to figure out what *confident* means. Next, read aloud and display the sentences and definitions from the Visual Model. Have students work in pairs. Ask one partner to reread a sentence aloud and have the other use context clues to determine the meaning of the underlined word. Have partners alternate roles for the other sentences. Then follow the suggestions in **Summarize/Reinforce.**

KINESTHETIC/MOTOR MODEL Write the example sentence from the Visual Model on the board and explain how to use context clues to figure out the meaning of the word *confident*. Circle each context clue. Distribute a copy of the sentences and definitions from the Visual Model to each student. Ask students to cut out the sentences and definitions and circle the context clues that helped them figure out the meanings of the underlined words. Have students match each definition with its corresponding sentence. Then follow the suggestions in **Summarize/Reinforce**

Summarize/Reinforce

Have students summarize what they learned. (When you come to an unfamiliar word, use the other words in the sentence to help figure out its meaning.) To reinforce the lesson, have students share some unfamiliar words they have encountered recently and tell how they used context to figure out the meanings. Remind students to use the strategies from this lesson when they come across unfamiliar words as they read.

Play

OBJECTIVE: *To understand and appreciate the elements of a play*

Focus

Share with students the following information:

> A *play* is a story that is written to be performed. A play has special elements that make it different from a story: Every time they speak, the *characters' names* are written. The author of a play often includes *stage directions,* or instructions that tell how the characters should move or speak. These instructions are included in brackets or parentheses. A play is divided into *scenes.* Recognizing the elements of a play helps students better understand and enjoy the plays they read.

Choose a Teaching Model

VISUAL MODEL Provide each student with a copy of the first page of a scene from a play. The page should include a description of the scene, dialogue involving two or more characters, and stage directions in brackets or parentheses. Write the following questions on the board: *Where does this scene take place? Who is the first character to speak? What other characters speak? What are the first stage directions?* Have students answer each question by writing notes on their copies. Ask volunteers to share their answers and to show where they found the information. Then follow the suggestions in **Summarize/Reinforce**.

AUDITORY MODEL Provide students with copies of the first page of a scene from a play. The page should include a description of the scene, dialogue involving two or more characters, and stage directions in brackets or parentheses. Have students follow along while you read the dialogue aloud. Then ask the questions listed in the Visual Model, and have volunteers respond orally. For questions focusing on the setting or on stage directions, ask students to identify where they found the answers. Have them read the stage directions aloud. Then follow the suggestions in **Summarize/Reinforce**.

KINESTHETIC/MOTOR MODEL Have students form small groups, and provide each group with a copy of a different scene from a play. Write the following terms on the board, and have students label one example of each element on their own copies: *character's name, stage direction, scene,* and *character's words.* Then have each group perform the scene for the class. If necessary, assist them in choosing parts. Each group may want to choose a director and a stage or technical manager as well as actors. Encourage group members to gather props, and allow time for rehearsal. Have each group present its scene to the rest of the class. Then follow the suggestions in **Summarize/Reinforce**.

Summarize/Reinforce

Check understanding of the lesson by having students summarize what they have learned. (A play is a story that is meant to be performed. The characters' names are written each time they speak. The author gives stage directions that are included in brackets or parentheses. A play is divided into scenes.) You may want to reinforce the lesson by having students perform a play for another class. Remind students to use their understanding of this lesson to help them enjoy reading plays.

GRAMMAR RETEACH

Object Pronouns

OBJECTIVE: *To recognize and use object pronouns*

Focus

Share with students the following information:

> An *object pronoun* replaces a noun after an action verb or a word such as *about, at, for, from, near, of, to,* and *with*. The words *me, you, him, her, it, us,* and *them* are object pronouns. Recognizing object pronouns helps readers better understand what they read.

Choose a Teaching Model

VISUAL MODEL Display the word box and paragraph. Also distribute a copy of the paragraph to each student.

| it | him | her | us | them | you | me |

Arthur found a gold ring. He gave _____ to his sister. Arthur gave _____ the ring because it was Daisy's birthday. Later, George came by and said the ring belonged to _____. Arthur and Daisy handed _____ the ring. George thanked _____. "I think I will give the ring to _____ anyway, Daisy, because it is your birthday," said George.

Have students fill in each blank with an object pronoun from the box. Then have them write the word or words each object pronoun replaces. Finally, ask them to circle the word that comes before each object pronoun and to tell whether it is an action verb or another word. Challenge students to write two sentences using the object pronouns *us* and *me*. Then follow the suggestions in **Summarize/Reinforce**.

AUDITORY MODEL Distribute to each student the paragraph and the word box from the Visual Model. Have students work in pairs to take turns reading aloud a sentence, pausing at the blank, and then replacing the blank with an object pronoun and rereading the sentence. Ask volunteers to share their answers by reading aloud the sentences with object pronouns in place. Also have students tell which word(s) the object pronoun replaces. Next, ask students to circle and name the word that precedes each object pronoun and to identify it as an action verb or other kind of word. Challenge students to write two additional sentences using the object pronouns *us* and *me*. Ask volunteers to read their sentences aloud. Then follow the suggestions in **Summarize/Reinforce**.

KINESTHETIC/MOTOR MODEL Distribute to pairs of students a "word box" and the paragraph from the Visual Model. Have partners copy each of the seven object pronouns onto separate index cards and put them into the word box. Then have one partner read aloud a sentence. The other partner should hold up the card with the object pronoun that belongs in the sentence. The partner who is reading should write the answers. Have partners switch roles after each sentence. Then ask students to identify the word(s) each object pronoun replaces. Finally, challenge students to write two original sentences using the words *us* and *me*. Ask volunteers to read their sentences aloud. Then follow the suggestions in **Summarize/Reinforce**.

Summarize/Reinforce

Check understanding of the lesson by having students summarize what they have learned. (*Me, you, him, her, it, us,* and *them* are object pronouns. Object pronouns replace a noun after an action verb or words such as *about, at, for, from, near, of, to,* and *with.*) You may want to reinforce the lesson by having students identify three object pronouns in a recent reading assignment. Remind students to use the information from this lesson to help them understand how object pronouns are used in sentences and to figure out what nouns they stand for or replace.

Fiction and Nonfiction

OBJECTIVE: *To distinguish fiction from nonfiction and mystery stories from other types of fiction*

Focus

Share with students the following information:

Fiction **tells about people, things, and events an author creates from his or her imagination. Mystery stories are one kind of fiction. In a mystery story, the characters use clues to try to solve a puzzle, and readers do not know what will happen next.** *Nonfiction* **tells about real people, places, things, or events. Knowing the difference between fiction and nonfiction helps students understand what they read.**

Choose a Teaching Model

VISUAL MODEL Make available a collection of library books that includes fiction, mysteries, and nonfiction. Have students work in pairs to find at least one example of a fiction, nonfiction, and mystery book. Write the following chart on the board, and model how to fill it in for "Piggins," as shown. Then have pairs of students copy the chart and complete it for each book they identified. Have them write how they know the book is fiction, nonfiction, or a mystery.

Book Title	Type	How I Know
Piggins	mystery	The characters use clues to solve a puzzle

When all pairs have identified at least one book for each category, ask volunteers to share their charts. Then follow the suggestions in **Summarize/Reinforce**.

AUDITORY MODEL Have on hand several library books with book-jacket summaries that show these books to be examples of fiction, nonfiction, and mysteries. Read aloud each summary, and ask students to write whether the book is fiction, nonfiction, or a mystery, along with how they know. Have volunteers share their answers. Discuss the characteristics that helped students find the answers. Then follow the suggestions in **Summarize/Reinforce**.

KINESTHETIC/MOTOR MODEL Have students work in small groups and look through student book-club flyers or the classroom or school library to find examples of fiction, nonfiction, and mystery books. Have each group member choose a book from one of these categories to present to the class. Have students discuss why the books they selected fit into the different categories. Then have each group present their books. Each student should give a short speech similar to the following: *The title of this book is _____. It is a _____ book. I know it is a _____ book because _____.* Have students point to the parts that helped them identify the type of book. Then follow the suggestions in **Summarize/Reinforce**.

Summarize/Reinforce

Check understanding of the lesson by having students summarize what they have learned. (Fiction tells about people, things, and events an author creates from his or her imagination. Mystery stories are a form of fiction in which the reader is held in suspense until the story characters solve a puzzle. Nonfiction tells about real-life topics.) You may want to reinforce the lesson by having students identify recently read books as fiction, nonfiction, or mysteries. Remind students to use the information from this lesson to help them understand and appreciate what they read.

GRAMMAR
RETEACH

Adjectives

OBJECTIVE: *To recognize and use adjectives*

Focus

Share the following information with students:

> An *adjective* is a word that describes a noun. Some adjectives tell *how many* and others tell *what kind.* Most adjectives come before the nouns they tell about. Being able to recognize and understand adjectives helps readers create a clearer mental picture of the people, places, things, and events they read about.

Choose a Teaching Model

VISUAL MODEL Display the following paragraph, omitting the underlining:

> We camped by the <u>peaceful</u> lake for <u>three</u> days. In the morning I sat on a <u>big</u> boulder near the campsite. I watched the <u>golden</u> sunrise. <u>Two</u> mornings in a row, my father caught <u>fresh</u> fish for breakfast. But <u>one</u> morning we had to eat <u>cold</u> macaroni! "I could stay here forever," I told my father. "It is a <u>beautiful</u> place," he agreed.

Have students read the paragraph silently and list all the adjectives in the paragraph on a separate sheet of paper. Next, have students pair off and rewrite these adjectives in two lists: one of adjectives that tell *how many,* and one of adjectives that tell *what kind.* Ask volunteers to write their lists on the board. Then have each student write two original sentences about a special place they have visited or that they can imagine, using the adjectives on the board, or others they think of on their own. Have volunteers write their sentences on the board and underline the adjectives. Then follow the suggestions in **Summarize/Reinforce**.

AUDITORY MODEL Display the passage from the Visual Model, and read it aloud. Organize students into two groups, one to listen for adjectives that tell *how many,* and one to listen for adjectives that tell *what kind.* Have them raise their hands when they hear one of "their" adjectives, and be prepared to identify it. Then have students orally compose sentences about a special place, using the adjectives from the board or adjectives they think of on their own. Have the two groups listen and identify the adjectives. Then follow the suggestions in **Summarize/Reinforce**.

KINESTHETIC/MOTOR MODEL Duplicate and distribute the paragraph from the Visual Model. Have students read the paragraph silently and underline the adjectives. When they are finished, have them work with a partner to check each other's work. Then ask students to cut out each adjective. Have them use these adjectives in their own sentences about a special place. Ask them to write on one side of a separate sheet of paper sentences with adjectives that tell *how many* and on the other side sentences using adjectives that tell *what kind.* Have volunteers share their work. Then follow the suggestions in **Summarize/Reinforce**.

Summarize/Reinforce

Check students' understanding of the lesson by having them summarize what they learned. (Adjectives are words that describe nouns or pronouns. Some adjectives tell *how many;* some adjectives tell *what kind.*) You may want to reinforce the lesson by having students identify and classify adjectives in other sources, and by having them use these adjectives in original sentences. Remind students that being able to understand and use adjectives will help them create a clearer picture of what they read and write.

VOCABULARY RETEACH

Synonyms/Antonyms/Analogies

OBJECTIVE: *To recognize analogies through the use of synonyms and antonyms*

Focus

Share with students the following information:

Synonyms are words that are similar in meaning. *Antonyms* are words that have opposite meanings. An *analogy* is made up of two pairs of words. Each pair is related in the same way. Antonyms and synonyms can be used in analogies. For example, *light* is to *dark* as *hot* is to *cold* is an analogy that uses antonyms. Knowing how words are related helps readers better understand what they read.

Choose a Teaching Model

VISUAL MODEL List pairs of synonyms and antonyms such as *silly/goofy, mad/angry, friend/pal, dark/gloomy, happy/cheerful, up/down, high/low, fast/slow, front/back,* and *separate/together* in random order on the board. Call on students to come up and either circle a pair of synonyms or draw a box around a pair of antonyms. Then have each student copy an analogy sentence frame: _____ is to _____ as _____ is to _____. Invite students to choose two pairs of synonyms or two pairs of antonyms and rewrite them as an analogy. Call on students to read their analogies to their classmates. Repeat the procedure until students have written several analogies. Then follow the suggestions in **Summarize/Reinforce.**

AUDITORY MODEL Read aloud the pairs of words from the Visual Model, and have students hold up one hand if they hear antonyms and both hands if they hear synonyms. Then print the following analogy sentence frame on the board: _____ is to _____ as _____ is to _____. Call on a student to name two synonyms. Write those in the first two blanks of the analogy sentence. Have the same student name two other synonyms. Write those to complete the analogy, and have students repeat it aloud. Repeat with another student, asking for antonyms. Continue until all students have had an opportunity to make an analogy. Then follow the suggestions in **Summarize/Reinforce.**

KINESTHETIC/MOTOR MODEL Write on the board the synonym and antonym pairs from the Visual Model. Have volunteers come to the front and write an *S* next to each synonym pair and an *A* next to each antonym pair. Give each student two different-colored cards, such as orange and yellow. Have students write a pair of synonyms on both sides of the orange cards and a pair of antonyms on both sides of the yellow cards. Then have pairs of students make a large sentence analogy strip, similar to the one below, that has blanks where the word cards can fit: _____ is to _____ as _____ is to _____. Have students take turns placing their cards in the sentence strip to make analogies. Call on students to read their analogies aloud. Then follow the suggestions in **Summarize/Reinforce.**

Summarize/Reinforce

Check understanding of the lesson by having students summarize what they have learned. (Synonyms are similar in meaning. Antonyms have opposite meanings. Analogies are made up of two pairs of words that are related in the same way. Antonyms and synonyms can be used in analogies.) You may want to reinforce the lesson by having students find synonyms and antonyms in stories they have read and then use them to create analogies. Remind students to use what they have learned to help them better understand the word relationships they encounter.

LIBRARY AND ADDITIONAL READINGS

The Harcourt Brace Library Books provide a collection of outstanding trade books that extend and enhance the unit themes in the Student Anthologies. Information about additional books suggested throughout the program is also provided.

CROSS-CURRICULAR CONNECTIONS • READING • LANGUAGE ARTS **UNIT 1 LIBRARY** CROSS-CURRICULAR CONNECTIONS • READING • LANGUAGE ARTS • CROS

Being Special

A Place to Dream

What are ways in which each person is special? The books *The Adventures of Ali Baba Bernstein* and *My Name Is María Isabel*, both *Harcourt Brace Library Books,* offer additional reading for students to enjoy as they further explore this theme.

The Adventures of Ali Baba Bernstein
by Johanna Hurwitz

ABOUT THE BOOK When eight-year-old David Bernstein discovers there are four Davids in his third-grade class, he decides to change his name. Inspired by the book *The Arabian Nights,* he calls himself Ali Baba Bernstein. Students will enjoy the exciting and humorous adventures that happen to Ali Baba throughout the book, and the startling discovery he makes about his real name.

THEME CONNECTION As students read this book, encourage them to think about what makes a person special. Ask whether they think the person's name is an important part of his or her personality.

My Name Is María Isabel
by Alma Flor Ada

ABOUT THE BOOK Third-grader María Isabel was born in Puerto Rico. She is now living in the United States, and she badly wants to fit in at school and yet keep her identity. When her teacher gives a writing assignment, "My Greatest Wish," María Isabel uses the assignment to fulfill her wish.

THEME CONNECTION Before students read this book, ask them to think about the special qualities María Isabel has. Encourage them to discuss whether it is always necessary to "fit in" with others.

For creative teaching ideas for independent and cooperative reading of *The Adventures of Ali Baba Bernstein* and *My Name Is María Isabel,* see the *Harcourt Brace Library Teacher's Guide* that accompanies each book.

Theme-Related Books in PASSPORTS

I Have Another Language: The Language Is Dance
   by Eleanor Schick

Mozart Tonight
   by Julie Downing

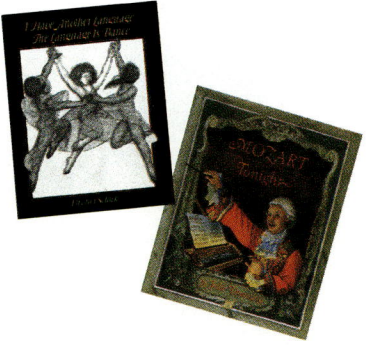

A PLACE TO DREAM

HARCOURT BRACE LIBRARY BOOKS / R39

UNIT 2 LIBRARY

Friendships

A Place to Dream

Over the years, children learn to enjoy many different kinds of friendships. The books *Ramona Quimby, Age 8* and *Ty's One-Man Band*, both *Harcourt Brace Library Books,* offer additional reading for students to enjoy as they further explore this theme.

Ramona Quimby, Age 8
by Beverly Cleary

ABOUT THE BOOK Ramona Quimby, now eight years old, arrives at her third-grade classroom to find a teacher who addresses the class as "you guys." At home she has to adjust to changes, too. Her mother goes to work while her father goes back to school. This humorous tale will delight students, who may find something of themselves within its pages.

THEME CONNECTION In this unit, students have read about many different kinds of friendships. After students read this book, ask them to talk about the various kinds of friendships the book depicts.

Ty's One-Man Band
by Mildred Pitts Walter

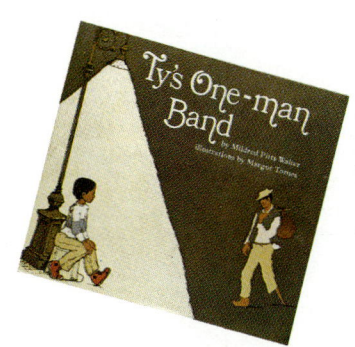

ABOUT THE BOOK During the hottest part of summer, Ty is bored—at least until he meets Andro, a peg-legged man who calls himself a "one-man band." This book creates mental pictures of hot, lazy summer days and reminds us of the fun people can have with simple, everyday things.

THEME CONNECTION After students read this book, ask them to tell about the friendships that evolved in the story.

For creative teaching ideas for independent and cooperative reading of *Ramona Quimby, Age 8* and *Ty's One-Man Band,* see the *Harcourt Brace Library Teacher's Guide* that accompanies each book.

Theme-Related Books in PASSPORTS

Julian's Glorious Summer
   by Ann Cameron

Mister King
   by Raija Siekkinen

Ramona Forever
   by Beverly Cleary

UNIT 3 LIBRARY

Adventures

A Place to Dream

Whether realistic or fantastic, adventure stories are perennial favorites of children. The books *Picnic with Piggins* and *Mush! Across Alaska in the World's Longest Sled-Dog Race,* both *Harcourt Brace Library Books,* offer additional reading for students to enjoy as they explore this theme further.

Picnic with Piggins
by Jane Yolen

ABOUT THE BOOK Piggins, the pig who serves as butler to the Reynard family, goes on a picnic in the country. During the picnic, a mystery develops. When solved, the mystery turns out to be a birthday surprise for Piggins.

THEME CONNECTION As students read this book, remind them to think about the adventures Piggins has. Encourage them to discuss ways in which his adventures are similar to those that students have read about elsewhere.

Mush! Across Alaska in the World's Longest Sled-Dog Race
by Patricia Seibert

ABOUT THE BOOK This informative book transports students to the icy state of Alaska for the world's longest sled-dog race. In addition to describing the race, this book paints a vivid and accurate background for students who may never have been so far north.

THEME CONNECTION What adventures might happen in a sled-dog race through the icy cold winter in Alaska? After students read this book, ask them to think of other adventures that might occur.

For creative teaching ideas for independent and cooperative reading of *Picnic with Piggins* and *Mush! Across Alaska in the World's Longest Sled-Dog Race,* see the *Harcourt Brace Library Teacher's Guide* that accompanies each book.

Theme-Related Books in PASSPORTS

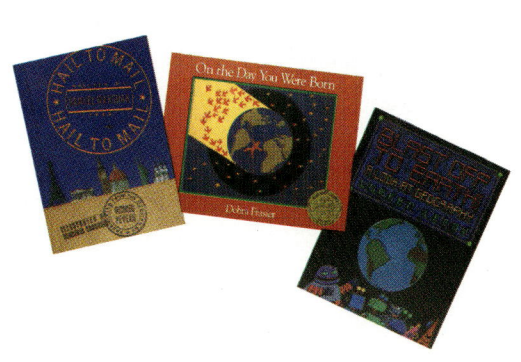

Hail to Mail
    by Samuel Yakovlevich Marshak

On the Day You Were Born
    by Debra Frasier

Blast Off to Earth: A Look at Geography
    by Loreen Leedy

UNIT 1 LIBRARY

Creatures

Sea of Wonder

Stories about animals are always popular among children; in fact, many of the stories children make up are about animals. The books *Animal Fact/Animal Fable* and *The Stories Julian Tells,* both *Harcourt Brace Library Books,* offer informative and amusing reading for students to enjoy as they further explore this theme.

Animal Fact/Animal Fable
by Seymour Simon

ABOUT THE BOOK In the most entertaining way possible, this book dispels many myths about animals and explains why other common beliefs are true. On every other page, the author presents a common belief about an animal. The reader can guess whether the belief is fact or fiction and then turn the page to find out.

THEME CONNECTION Students have read about many types of animals in "Creatures." Have them think of other common beliefs that they may have heard about those animals or about other animals.

The Stories Julian Tells
by Ann Cameron

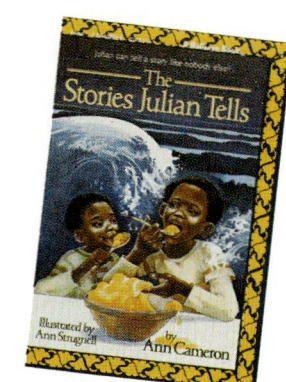

ABOUT THE BOOK The stories Julian tells his younger brother, Huey, are nothing if not imaginative. When their father orders a garden catalog, Julian spins a tale about the cats they can order from the catalog. In this and four other episodes, the author entertains with lighthearted humor that will delight students.

THEME CONNECTION After students read this book, have them tell about animal stories they may have created to entertain brothers, sisters, or friends.

For creative teaching ideas for independent and cooperative reading of *Animal Fact/Animal Fable* and *The Stories Julian Tells,* see the *Harcourt Brace Library Teacher's Guide* that accompanies each book.

Theme-Related Books in PASSPORTS

Lorenzo the Naughty Parrot
　　by Tony Johnston

In the Eyes of the Cat: Japanese Poetry for All Seasons
　　edited and illustrated by Demi

UNIT 2 LIBRARY

Puzzlers

We face different types of "puzzlers" every day. The books *Rainy Rainy Saturday* and *The Magic Fan,* both *Harcourt Brace Library Books,* offer additional reading for students to enjoy as they further explore this theme.

Rainy Rainy Saturday
by Jack Prelutsky

ABOUT THE BOOK This collection of fourteen humorous poems describes the pleasures and pains of a rainy Saturday.

THEME CONNECTION Sometimes, what to do on a rainy Saturday can be the biggest "puzzler" of all. After students read this book, have them talk about other things they could do on a rainy Saturday. Also discuss how the book and the selections about weather in the Student Anthology are alike and different.

The Magic Fan
by Keith Baker

ABOUT THE BOOK In a Japanese village, a young carpenter who finds inspiration to create new and beautiful things from a magic fan helps villagers overcome their resistance to the unfamiliar. Along the way, the carpenter discovers his own creativity.

THEME CONNECTION After students read this book, encourage them to tell about the puzzles that face the young carpenter.

For creative teaching ideas for independent and cooperative reading of *Rainy Rainy Saturday* and *The Magic Fan,* see the *Harcourt Brace Library Teacher's Guide* that accompanies each book.

Theme-Related Books in PASSPORTS

Sebastian (Super Sleuth) and the Crummy Yummies Caper
    by Mary Blount Christian

The Sly Spy
    by Marjorie Weinman-Sharmat and Mitchell Sharmat

Peter and the Wolf
    by Michèle Lemieux

A PLACE TO DREAM

UNIT 3 LIBRARY

Memories

What can the past teach us? What part do memories play in our lives? The books *The News About Dinosaurs* and *The Keeping Quilt,* both *Harcourt Brace Library Books,* offer additional reading for students to enjoy as they further explore this theme.

The News About Dinosaurs
by Patricia Lauber

ABOUT THE BOOK The study of a wide variety of dinosaurs, with information about their appearance, habits, and habitats, is the focus of this nonfiction book. Full-color illustrations help present an accurate vision of what is currently known about dinosaurs.

THEME CONNECTION Before students read this book, ask them to think about how scientists find out about dinosaurs, creatures of the distant past.

The Keeping Quilt
by Patricia Polacco

ABOUT THE BOOK When Great Gramma Anna came to America from Russia as a child, she did not have much to remind her of the old ways. Her mother took pieces of worn-out clothing and made a quilt to remind the family of the old country. This story traces the quilt and its uses through four generations.

THEME CONNECTION As students read this book, have them think of all the memories that the quilt held for the people who used it. Encourage students to think of something they could make that would hold memories.

For creative teaching ideas for independent and cooperative reading of *The News About Dinosaurs* and *The Keeping Quilt,* see the *Harcourt Brace Library Teacher's Guide* that accompanies each book.

Theme-Related Books in PASSPORTS

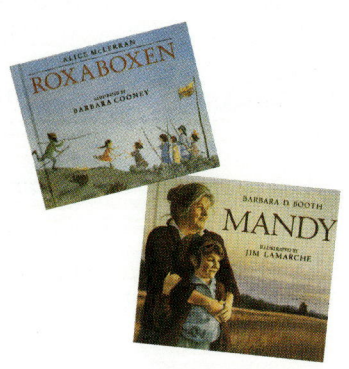

Roxaboxen
    by Alice McLerran

Mandy
    by Barbara D. Booth

UNIT 1 ADDITIONAL READING

Being Special

The following list is a compilation of the additional reading suggestions from the lesson plans.

THEME: Planting a Seed

Chanticleer and the Fox by Barbara Cooney, adapted from *The Canterbury Tales*. HarperCollins, 1982. **CHALLENGING**
Cooney's charming illustrations of pompous Chanticleer and the clever fox enhance a lyrical adaptation of Chaucer's "The Nun's Priest's Tale." CALDECOTT MEDAL

Frederick by Leo Lionni. Alfred A. Knopf, 1987. **EASY**
All the other mice busily gather food for winter, but Frederick dreams lazily and gathers only the sun's rays. When winter comes, Frederick shows that he has gathered things that are just as important as food: the glow of the sun, the colors of nature, and the words of poetry. CALDECOTT HONOR, *NEW YORK TIMES* BEST ILLUSTRATED BOOKS OF THE YEAR

Green Thumbs Up! The Science of Growing Plants by Barbara Taylor. Random House, 1992. **CHALLENGING**
This excellent book for young gardeners provides concise information about all the needs of growing plants. An index is included. OUTSTANDING SCIENCE TRADE BOOK

Greening the City Streets by Barbara A. Huff. Clarion, 1990. **CHALLENGING**
Children and adults living in large cities discover the joy and practicality of growing beautiful flowering vegetable gardens. They "green" the alleys and abandoned lots in the process.

Hattie and the Wild Waves: A Story from Brooklyn by Barbara Cooney. Viking, 1990. **AVERAGE**
Set in Brooklyn and Long Island, this gentle story from an earlier era tells of a young girl's love of painting, the home and family that she grows up in, and the beautiful seaside that she visits.

Henry Bear's Park by David McPhail. Little, Brown, 1976. **AVERAGE**
Henry loves being superintendent of his father's park when his father leaves on a balloon adventure. But after a while Henry begins to miss his father terribly.

How Trees Help Me by Bobbie Kalman and Janine Schaub. Crabtree, 1992. **AVERAGE**
Color photos enhance this concise text, which tells how trees grow and why they are important to us. Students will be intrigued by "How to Troll a Tree." A glossary and an index are included.

The Island of the Skog by Steven Kellogg. Dial, 1976. **AVERAGE**
Hoping to find a place free of cats, dogs, and other urban hazards, a group of mice sail away. They land on an island inhabited by one Skog and set out to trap it. AWARD-WINNING AUTHOR

John Muir: Man of the Wild Places by Carol Greene. Children's Press, 1991. **EASY**
Early black-and-white photographs of Muir and contemporary color photos of natural scenes important in his life provide a striking, easy-to-read biography.

June 29, 1999 by David Weisner. Clarion, 1992. **EASY**
Budding scientist Holly Evans rockets vegetable seedlings into the sky above Ho-Ho-Kus, New Jersey, and is amazed at the results of her experiment. ALA NOTABLE BOOK, SLJ BEST BOOKS OF THE YEAR

Just a Dream by Chris Van Allsburg. Houghton Mifflin, 1990. **AVERAGE**
Walter cares little about the environment until in a dream he sees what the world would be like if everyone were to treat it as he does. The next day he goes back to pick up his litter, and he plants a tree for his birthday. AWARD-WINNING AUTHOR

The Legend of the Bluebonnet by Tomie dePaola. G. P. Putnam's Sons, 1983. **EASY**
This is a Comanche legend about a drought that will not end until the people make sacrifices of their most-prized possessions. A little girl gives up a doll, her only possession from her deceased parents.

The Life and Times of the Apple by Charles Micucci. Orchard, 1992. **AVERAGE**
This witty book tells all you need to know about raising apples. A concise text, a time line, and easy-to-follow graphs and drawings make the concepts understandable. ALA NOTABLE BOOK, OUTSTANDING SCIENCE TRADE BOOK

My First Garden Book: A Life-Size Guide to Growing Things at Home by Angela Wilkes. Alfred A. Knopf, 1992. **AVERAGE**
Children eager to garden will appreciate the easy-to-follow instructions in this book and the photographs that identify the tools they will need. OUTSTANDING SCIENCE TRADE BOOK

Pinkerton, Behave! by Steven Kellogg. Dial, 1982. **AVERAGE**
In this hilarious story with wonderful watercolor illustrations, poor Pinkerton not only gets all F's in obedience school but also disrupts the entire class. AWARD-WINNING AUTHOR

Prehistoric Pinkerton by Steven Kellogg. Puffin, 1991.
AVERAGE
Unfortunately, Pinkerton is teething when he accompanies his young owner and her class to Dinosaur Days at the museum of natural history. Soon the prized exhibit is in jeopardy and the museum is in chaos. AWARD-WINNING AUTHOR

Roxaboxen by Alice McLertan. Lothrop, Lee & Shepard, 1991.
AVERAGE
To others it may be just another rocky and sandy hill with old wooden boxes, but to the children it is a very special place.

The Tree of Here by Chaim Potok. Alfred A. Knopf, 1993.
AVERAGE
When his family has to move, a boy finds it very hard to leave his friend the dogwood tree. But as he and his family are leaving, his neighbor, Mr. Healy, brings him a surprise.

Uncle Willie and the Soup Kitchen by Dyanne DiSalvo-Ryan. William Morrow, 1991. **AVERAGE**
A young boy wonders why his Uncle Willie volunteers in a soup kitchen, until the boy spends his own day off helping out. NOTABLE CHILDREN'S TRADE BOOK IN SOCIAL STUDIES

THEME: Being Different

A, My Name Is Alice by Jane Bayer. Dial, 1984. **EASY**
As in the traditional ball-bouncing and jump-rope rhyme, each letter of the alphabet is chanted with names and words that begin with the letter.

Aldo Peanut Butter by Johanna Hurwitz. William Morrow, 1990. **CHALLENGING**
The Sossi children try to housebreak Peanut and Butter, the new puppies, and cope with the complaints of crabby Mrs. Crosby during two hilarious weeks while their parents are away.

Daddy Has a Pair of Striped Shorts by Mimi Otey. Farrar, Straus & Giroux, 1990. **EASY**
Although Daddy is loved by his family and by his African American congregation, his unusual clothing combinations often embarrass his daughter. NOTABLE CHILDREN'S TRADE BOOK IN SOCIAL STUDIES

Dancing Teepees: Poems of American Indian Youth
selected by Virginia Driving Hawk Sneve. Holiday House, 1989. **CHALLENGING**
These poetic selections include prayers, lullabies, and songs that are deeply important to Native Americans. ALA NOTABLE BOOK

Emily by Michael Bedard. Doubleday, 1992. **AVERAGE**
The reclusive poet Emily Dickinson is the subject of this beautifully illustrated, mysterious story set in nineteenth-century Amherst, Massachusetts. ALA NOTABLE BOOK

Hurray for Ali Baba Bernstein by Johanna Hurwitz. Scholastic, 1990. **CHALLENGING**
Ali Baba continues his quest for the unusual by checking on the mysterious movements of a neighbor, finding royalty on a shopping trip, and asking Santa Claus some questions he has as a Jewish nonreceiver of Santa's gifts. AWARD-WINNING AUTHOR

I Have Another Language: The Language Is Dance
by Eleanor Schick. Macmillan, 1992. **EASY**
This story is about a young girl who is preparing for her first dance performance before an audience. While performing, she learns a new language without words, the language of dance.

I Took My Frog to the Library by Eric Kimmel. Viking, 1990. **EASY**
Each day, a young girl brings a different pet when she visits the library, and the results are disastrous. Different parts of the library and activities at the library are referred to.

Loving by Ann Morris. Lothrop, Lee & Shepard, 1990. **EASY**
Bright color photos of different ethnic groups show the many ways in which children and their families express their love. NOTABLE CHILDREN'S TRADE BOOK IN SOCIAL STUDIES

Walden text selected by Steve Lowe. Philomel, 1990. **AVERAGE**
Henry David Thoreau lived on Walden Pond, where he wrote about his life. These excerpts describe Thoreau's experiences filled with the wonders of nature.

THEME: Listen to This!

Alligators and Music by Donald Elliott. Gambit, 1976.
AVERAGE
This informational book introduces the instruments of the orchestra—strings, woodwinds, brasses, percussion, and others—in a unique way: alligators are depicted playing the instruments. This feature helps make learning about the orchestra quite entertaining.

Caribbean Carnival: Songs of the West Indies by Irving Burgie. Tambourine, 1992. **EASY**
Vividly colored illustrations enhance this book of familiar songs from the West Indies. Included are "Day-o," "Michael Row the Boat Ashore," and "Yellow Bird." NOTABLE CHILDREN'S TRADE BOOK IN SOCIAL STUDIES

A Chair for My Mother by Vera B. Williams. William Morrow, 1988. **AVERAGE**
When a fire destroys the family's home, friends contribute basic household items. But Rosa, Mama, and Grandma all want a special chair, so they begin to save their coins in a big jar. CALDECOTT HONOR, BOSTON GLOBE-HORN BOOK AWARD, ALA NOTABLE BOOK

Chin Chiang and the Dragon's Dance by Ian Wallace. Macmillan, 1984. **CHALLENGING**
Chin Chiang dreams of dancing the dragon's dance, but when the time comes he is afraid and hides. After Pu Wee comes to his rescue, Chin Chiang dances and makes his grandfather proud. IBBY HONOR LIST

***Cynthia Gregory Dances* Swan Lake** by Cynthia Gregory. Simon & Schuster, 1990. **AVERAGE**
The glamour and excitement of a dancing career are clearly evident as the famous ballerina describes a day in her life, which begins with a workout and ends with a triumphant performance of *Swan Lake*.

Fishy Facts by Ivan Chermayeff. Harcourt Brace, 1994. **EASY**
As the title implies, this is a fun, informational book about various types of fish, with wonderful illustrations to match. If you have never heard of a parrotfish, a goosefish, a lantern fish, or a cowfish, to mention just a few, then you will enjoy learning about their unique characteristics.

Gonna Sing My Head Off!: American Folk Songs for Children collected and arranged by Kathleen Krull. Alfred A. Knopf, 1992. **AVERAGE**
This entertaining and beautifully illustrated book presents a musical history of America through favorite American folk songs. NOTABLE CHILDREN'S TRADE BOOK IN SOCIAL STUDIES

Grandpa's Song by Tony Johnston. Dial, 1991. **AVERAGE**
Warm watercolor illustrations contribute to this story about children helping out Grandpa when he forgets the words to his song. NOTABLE CHILDREN'S TRADE BOOK IN SOCIAL STUDIES

Mozart Tonight by Julie Downing. Bradbury, 1991. **AVERAGE**
This picture-book biography of Mozart tells about the composer's early passion for music and his brief but glorious career in Vienna. NOTABLE CHILDREN'S TRADE BOOK IN SOCIAL STUDIES

The Musical Life of Gustave Mole by Katherine Meyrick. Child's Play, 1990. **AVERAGE**
Humorous illustrations present Gustave and the Mole family and their all-animal orchestra. Mother Mole shows how to make instruments from everyday objects.

Peter and the Wolf retold by Selina Hastings. Henry Holt, 1990. **AVERAGE**
Richly colored paintings of snowy scenes illustrate this retelling of Sergei Prokofiev's tale for introducing the orchestra.

Red Dancing Shoes by Denise Lewis Patrick. William Morrow, 1993. **EASY**
Grandmama's present to her granddaughter is a pair of the reddest and shiniest shoes—red dancing shoes. The girl feels that these shoes are magical. But when she goes to show her shoes to her favorite aunt, she falls in the mud and the shoes become dirty. How can she get the magic and the shine back into her shoes?

Something Special for Me by Vera B. Williams. William Morrow, 1986. **AVERAGE**
Rosa and her mother empty the jar once again and go from store to store searching for the perfect birthday present for Rosa. AWARD-WINNING AUTHOR

A Very Young Musician by Jill Krementz. Simon & Schuster, 1991. **CHALLENGING**
Krementz's wonderful full-color photos tell an engaging story about gifted Josh Broder, a young man who plays a terrific trumpet. AWARD-WINNING AUTHOR

What Instrument Is This? by Rosmarie Hausherr. Scholastic, 1992. **AVERAGE**
This unique photo essay shows readers that making music is fun. A question such as "What instrument is played through a bag filled with air?" appears beneath a photo of a child holding the instrument. A brief, well-written answer appears opposite the photo.

UNIT 2 ADDITIONAL READING

The following list is a compilation of the additional reading suggestions from the lesson plans.

Friendships

THEME: School Days

Anno's Math Games by Mitsumasa Anno. Philomel, 1987.
AVERAGE
Kriss and Kross lead the reader through problems that show how to compare, contrast, break apart, and combine parts of a whole. An excellent book for teaching children to observe closely.
ALA NOTABLE BOOK

Best Friends by Steven Kellogg. Dial, 1986. **EASY**
Louise goes to camp for the summer, and Kathy stays home. Jealousy emerges when a spotted puppy is promised to Kathy, but only a brown one is born and is given to Louise. The two girls resolve their feelings through Louise's generosity.

The Candy Corn Contest by Patricia Reilly Giff. Dell, 1984.
EASY
Richard Best's teacher, Ms. Rooney, has a jar filled with candy corn on her desk, and whoever guesses the exact amount wins the candy. However, in order to earn a guess, Richard has to read a page in a library book, and he isn't a good reader. What happens when Richard eats three of the candies?

Chicken Sunday by Patricia Polacco. Philomel, 1992.
AVERAGE
Three children look forward to each Sunday, when Miss Eula makes a chicken dinner after church. The children are mistakenly blamed for throwing eggs at the door to a hat shop. They eventually win the friendship of the owner and raise money to buy the beautiful hat Miss Eula has admired. NOTABLE CHILDREN'S TRADE BOOK IN SOCIAL STUDIES

Henry and the Paper Route by Beverly Cleary.
William Morrow, 1957. **CHALLENGING**
To attract customers for his paper route, Henry tries several enterprising schemes, such as giving away free kittens. But it is Ramona Quimby who saves the day. AWARD-WINNING AUTHOR

The Hot and Cold Summer by Johanna Hurwitz. Scholastic, 1985. **CHALLENGING**
A contemporary story of a girl and two boys, dealing with the "hot" and "cold" aspects of their friendship during a summer.
AWARD-WINNING AUTHOR

How a Book Is Made by Aliki. HarperCollins, 1988.
AVERAGE
Aliki's entertaining drawings show how a book is made, beginning with the author's idea and ending with the marketing of the bound product.

I Can Be a Biologist by Paul P. Sipiera. Children's Press, 1992.
AVERAGE
Excellent photos of biologists at work enhance this concisely written text, which emphasizes how a biologist's work can save lives. A glossary and an index are included.

The Math Wiz by Betsy Duffey. Puffin, 1993. **AVERAGE**
Marty, the new boy in third grade, loves math but hates gym, which he constantly tries to get out of. Then a sympathetic teacher and a classmate reassure him that he's not alone.

Muggie Maggie by Beverly Cleary. Avon, 1991. **AVERAGE**
Maggie, a likable third-grader, is struggling to switch from printing to cursive handwriting in this charmingly realistic story about a kind family and believable school situations. AWARD-WINNING AUTHOR

Ramona Forever by Beverly Cleary. William Morrow, 1984.
CHALLENGING
Ramona's family life is shown through her eyes. Through all the ups and downs of everyday life, Ramona remains "wonderful, blunderful me." CHILDREN'S CHOICE

THEME: Caring and Sharing

And Still the Turtle Watched by Sheila MacGill-Callahan.
Dial, 1991. **CHALLENGING**
For years the stone-carved Turtle watches over the Delaware people. But eventually weather erodes Turtle, and children write on him with spray paint. Then a man who knows what Turtle stands for rescues him. NOTABLE CHILDREN'S TRADE BOOK IN SOCIAL STUDIES, OUTSTANDING SCIENCE TRADE BOOK

Blackberries in the Dark by Mavis Jukes. Alfred A. Knopf, 1993. **EASY**
Austin and his grandmother grieve in their own ways after his grandfather's death. Then several attempts at fly-fishing, one of the grandfather's favorite activities, bring them closer together.

Brave Irene by William Steig. Farrar, Straus & Giroux, 1988.
AVERAGE
Because her mother, a seamstress, is ill, Little Irene struggles through a raging snowstorm in order to deliver the fine gown that her mother has made for the Duchess. Irene's bravery is well rewarded. NEW YORK TIMES BEST ILLUSTRATED BOOK OF THE YEAR

Chicken Sunday by Patricia Polacco. Philomel, 1992.
AVERAGE
Three children look forward to each Sunday, when Miss Eula makes a chicken dinner after church. The children are mistakenly blamed for throwing eggs at the door to a hat shop. They eventually win the friendship of the owner and raise money to buy the beautiful hat Miss Eula has admired. NOTABLE CHILDREN'S TRADE BOOK IN SOCIAL STUDIES

Dora's Book by Michelle Edwards. Carolrhoda, 1990. **EASY**
Dora remembers her grandparents by writing a book about them. Tom, a printer, makes copies to give to her friends. This is a fine introduction to how a book is made.

The First Strawberries: A Cherokee Story retold by Joseph Bruchac. Dial, 1993. **EASY**
When Woman and Man have an argument, she decides to leave. He follows because he wants to say he's sorry for losing his temper. But he can't seem to catch up until Sun helps out.

Grandmama's Joy by Eloise Greenfield. Philomel, 1980.
CHALLENGING
This touching story shows that love is the most important factor in overcoming the sadness brought about by loss and change.
AWARD-WINNING AUTHOR

R48 / A PLACE TO DREAM

Happy Birthday Grampie by Susan Pearson. Dial, 1987. EASY

A little girl misses communicating with her nearly blind, elderly grandfather, who has reverted to speaking his native language, Swedish. Through a tactile birthday card, she is able to reestablish communication with him.

Here Comes the Mystery Man by Scott Russell Sanders. Bradbury, 1993. CHALLENGING

In the 1800s on a farm in the Midwest, a pioneer family eagerly waits for the peddler who brings not only goods to sell but also news to share from the rest of the country.

Loop the Loop by Barbara Dugan, Puffin, 1993. AVERAGE

Little Annie's new friend, Old Mrs. Simpson, is sharp and a whiz with a yo-yo. But then she breaks her hip, and everything changes. ALA NOTABLE BOOK, NOTABLE CHILDREN'S TRADE BOOK IN SOCIAL STUDIES

Magical Hands by Marjorie Barker. Picture Book Studios, 1991. EASY

William makes the birthdays of his three friends very special in this touching story of true friendship. Striking illustrations enhance the story.

Mama One, Mama Two by Patricia MacLachlan. HarperCollins, 1982. EASY

Mamma One becomes very depressed and must enter a hospital. But Maudie is lucky because Mama Two, her foster mother, treats her with love and understanding while Mama One is away. AWARD-WINNING AUTHOR

Mandy by Barbara Booth. Lothrop, Lee & Shepard, 1991. AVERAGE

Mandy is the story of the love between a young girl and her grandmother. They do many things together. Then something happens that forces Mandy to go outside on a dark, stormy night. TEACHER'S CHOICE

Mister King by Raija Siekkinen. Carolrhoda, 1986. AVERAGE

A lonely king's life changes when a very unusual cat visits the castle. AWARD-WINNING AUTHOR

Nana Upstairs and Nana Downstairs by Tomie dePaola. Puffin, 1978. EASY

The author's two grandmothers live with him during his childhood, one upstairs and one downstairs. The activities they share with him are lovingly described. He learns to cope with the death of Nana Upstairs. AWARD-WINNING AUTHOR

Three Names by Patricia MacLachlan. HarperCollins, 1991. AVERAGE

Three Names is a young boy's dog in this appealing story about a time when children on prairie farms went to school in a horse-drawn wagon. Three Names went along too, to show the way. AWARD-WINNING AUTHOR

The True Story of the Three Little Pigs by Jon Scieszka. Viking, 1989. EASY

A. Wolf tells the *real* story about the three little pigs. His tale involves Granny's birthday cake, a head cold, and a bad reputation. It ends in the Big House: the Pig Pen. You decide what really happened when A. Wolf appeared at the door. ALA NOTABLE BOOK

Wilfred Gordon McDonald Partridge by Mem Fox. Kane-Miller, 1989. EASY

Wilfred is worried when he hears his parents saying that Miss Nancy has lost her memory. He asks various residents of the "old people's home" what a memory is, and he assembles a collection of items to help Miss Nancy find her memory.

THEME: Learning About Yourself

The Cowboy and the Blackeyed Pea by Tony Johnston. G. P. Putnam's Sons, 1992. **AVERAGE**

In this Old West version of "The Princess and the Pea," a young woman is advised by her father to hide a black-eyed pea under the saddle blanket of any gentleman who asks for her hand. **AWARD-WINNING AUTHOR**

Different Dragons by Jean Little. Puffin, 1989. **CHALLENGING**

Ben is uneasy about visiting his aunt Rose. He is also nervous around animals, during thunderstorms, and with new people. But Ben learns that he is not the only one with fears.

Everyday Things and How They Work by Steve Parker. Random House, 1991. **AVERAGE**

In simple, concise language, this book explains how useful but ordinary items work, such as light bulbs, microwave ovens, and telecommunication networks.

Harry in Trouble by Barbara Ann Porte. Greenwillow, 1989. **EASY**

Harry is scared to admit that he has lost his library card for the third time. He is very surprised by the librarian's response when he finally confesses what happened.

Julian's Glorious Summer by Ann Cameron. Random House, 1987. **AVERAGE**

Julian is afraid of bicycles, but he doesn't want Gloria, who rides a bike skillfully, to know. Discover how Julian tries to keep bicycles out of his life. **ALA NOTABLE BOOK**

Mariah Loves Rock by Mildred Pitts Walter. Troll, 1989. **CHALLENGING**

Mariah's stepsister, her father's teenager daughter by a previous marriage, is going to move in, and Mariah's mother is very anxious about it. But Mariah is too fascinated by a rock star to face this change in her life.

Masai and I by Virginia Kroll. Four Winds, 1992. **EASY**

At school a little girl learns about the tall proud people called the Masai. She wonders how she would live if she were a Masia girl in East Africa.

Pecos Bill by Steven Kellogg. William Morrow, 1986. **AVERAGE**

The tall tale of Pecos Bill is told, from his childhood among the coyotes to his return to life among humans. Humorous incidents are related along the way. **NEWBERY HONOR**

Yonder by Tony Johnston. Puffin, 1991. **AVERAGE**

The simple cycle of farm life is revealed in this eloquent story. A farmer plants a plum tree "yonder" and a family begins. The years pass, children are born, and more plum trees are planted, which flourish along with the family. **NOTABLE CHILDREN'S TRADE BOOK IN SOCIAL STUDIES**

UNIT 3 ADDITIONAL READING

The following list is a compilation of the additional reading suggestions from the lesson plans.

Adventures

THEME: Picture This!

All I See by Cynthia Rylant. Orchard, 1988. **EASY**
This story is about a friendship between Charlie and Gregory, who is an artist. Charlie hides and watches Gregory in order to see what Gregory sees and paints. When Charlie sees the painting, he likes Gregory even better. AWARD-WINNING AUTHOR

The Art Lesson by Tomie de Paola. G. P. Putnam's Sons, 1989. **AVERAGE**
Tomie can hardly wait for his first real art lesson. But the lesson goes terribly wrong. He isn't allowed to use his own big box of crayons, and he is told to copy a picture. AWARD-WINNING AUTHOR

A Bear Called Paddington by Michael Bond. Houghton Mifflin, 1960. **AVERAGE**
Mr. and Mrs. Brown meet Paddington, a bear from Peru, in a train station in London. They take him into their home, not realizing that life will never be the same once Paddington becomes part of their family.

The Bunny Play by Loreen Leedy. Holiday House, 1988. **EASY**
A group of bunnies decides to put on a production of Little Red Riding Hood, and each bunny takes a part in producing it. The play is shown in illustrations, and a glossary of theater terms is included.

Colors by Philip Yenawine. Delacorte, 1991. **EASY**
This book teaches how each color is used by artists and the meaning of color in art. It shows how colors can convey feelings and is one of a series of books intended to help children learn the basics of art.

Eyes of the Dragon by Margaret Leaf. Lothrop, Lee & Shepard, 1987. **AVERAGE**
A Chinese magistrate decides to have a dragon painted on a wall being built around his village. This tale relates what happens when the magistrate breaks a historic law. ALA NOTABLE BOOK

The Girl Who Loved Wild Horses by Paul Goble. Bradbury, 1978. **AVERAGE**
This Native American tale is about a young girl who understands horses in a special way and eventually becomes one. CALDECOTT MEDAL

Harold and the Purple Crayon by Crockett Johnson. HarperCollins, 1981. **EASY**
Harold takes his purple crayon and becomes involved in the adventures that he draws.

The Hole in the Dike by Norma Green. Scholastic, 1993. **EASY**
This traditional story tells how a little boy saves his village from flooding when a hole appears in the dike.

Lines by Philip Yenawine. Delacorte, 1991. **EASY**
This book shows how lines are used by artists and the meaning of lines in art. It is one of a series of books intended to display some of the basics of art.

Michael the Angel by Laura Fischetto. Delacorte, 1993. **CHALLENGING**
Marvelous frescolike paintings, some humorous, enhance this story of the life and career of the great artist Michelangelo.

On the Day You Were Born by Debra Frasier. Harcourt Brace, 1991. **CHALLENGING**
This book celebrates the relationship between the earth and people. It is a song about the moon, the ocean, and all human life.

The Perfect Spot by Robert J. Blake. Philomel, 1992. **AVERAGE**
In this well-written and beautifully illustrated story, a father and his son explore the woods in search of the perfect spot for a day of painting. OUTSTANDING SCIENCE TRADE BOOK

The Popcorn Book by Tomie dePaola. Holiday House, 1978. **AVERAGE**
Twin brothers have a popcorn-making adventure. This book tells how to make popcorn, gives the history of this popular snack, and offers some delicious recipes. AWARD-WINNING AUTHOR

Rembrandt's Beret by Johnny Alcorn. Tambourine, 1991. **CHALLENGING**
To get his granddaughter to sit still while he paints her portrait, Grandfather describes a fantastic incident he experienced years ago. He accidentally became locked in the famous Uffizi Gallery, and the portraits of great artists came to life.

Shapes by Philip Yenawine. Delacorte, 1991. **EASY**
This book takes individual shapes and exhibits their use by artists and explains the meaning that shapes have in art. It is one of a series of books intended to help young people learn some of the basics of art.

Stories by Philip Yenawine. Delacorte, 1991. **EASY**
These compact and concise books offer superb introductions to the artist's use of color, line, and shape. They were originally published by New York City's Museum of Modern Art.

The Tales of Olga da Polga by Michael Bond. Macmillan, 1989. **CHALLENGING**
Olga da Polga is a guinea pig who leaves a pet shop to live with humans. She experiences many adventures and is incredibly good at telling tales. Her mixing of human attributes and those of guinea pigs provides an entertaining blend of realism and fantasy. ALA NOTABLE BOOK

Visiting the Art Museum by Laurene Krasny Brown and Marc Tolon Brown. E. P. Dutton, 1990. **AVERAGE**
Art-viewing tips are included in this lighthearted adventure, in which a family wanders through a museum, enjoying art from many different periods.

The Young Artist by Thomas Locker. Dial, 1989. **AVERAGE**
Illustrations reminiscent of sevententh-century Dutch paintings enhance this story about a gifted young artist who rejects portrait painting and turns to landscapes. NOTABLE CHILDREN'S TRADE BOOK IN SOCIAL STUDIES

THEME: Mysteries to Solve

All Those Secrets of the World by Jane Yolen. Little, Brown, 1991. **AVERAGE**
When Janie watches her Daddy's ship head out to sea, her cousin explains that it looks small because it's far away. When Daddy returns, Janie says she is big because Daddy is near. NOTABLE CHILDREN'S TRADE BOOK IN SOCIAL STUDIES

Commander Toad and the Intergalactic Spy by Jane Yolen. Coward-McCann, 1986. **AVERAGE**
This lively, easy-to-read story tells how Commander Toad searches for his cousin Tip Toad, who is also known as Agent 007 1/2. AWARD-WINNING AUTHOR

Dreamplace by George Ella Lyon. Orchard, 1993. **EASY**
Dreamlike illustrations help create a vision of what life was like among the Anasazi of Mesa Verde, who disappeared mysteriously. They left their dwellings but few clues to why they abandoned them.

If You Were a Writer by Joan Lowery Nixon. Four Winds, 1988. **AVERAGE**
A young girl asks her mother how she goes about her job as a writer. Several examples are used, and all are mystery stories. AWARD-WINNING AUTHOR

My Dog and the Green Sock Mystery by David A. Adler. Holiday House, 1986. **EASY**
Jenny's friend is missing some things. Amusing cartoonlike drawings enhance this story of how Jenny's dog looks for the missing items.

Nature Detective: How to Solve Outdoor Mysteries by Eileen M. Docekal. Sterling, 1991. **CHALLENGING**
In this book, children will find two hundred clues to help them investigate a backyard, a field, or a wooded area. They will also learn to appreciate wildlife they usually don't even notice.

Welcome to the Greenhouse by Jane Yolen. G. P. Putnam's Sons, 1983. **EASY**
This house has a canopy of branches instead of a roof. Its walls are the trunks of giant trees. Vividly colored plants and animals contrast with the greenery. This house is the rain forest. AWARD-WINNING AUTHOR

THEME: The Great Outdoors

Another Celebrated Dancing Bear by Gladys Scheffrin-Falk. Macmillan, 1991. **AVERAGE**
Hand-colored etchings enhance this story of Max, a famous dancing bear in the Moscow Circus who offers to give his friend Boris dancing lessons. Soon there are two celebrated dancing bears.

The Bicycle Man by Allen Say. Houghton Mifflin, 1989. **AVERAGE**
It's sports day at a small mountain school in Japan shortly after the end of World War II. Two tall American soldiers arrive, and, at first, the children are frightened. But soon everyone is laughing and cheering. ALA NOTABLE BOOK

Follow the Water from Brook to Ocean by Arthur Dorros. HarperCollins, 1991. **AVERAGE**
This interesting little book provides a clear description of where water comes from and where it goes, from rain to brook to ocean.

Grandfather's Journey by Allen Say. Houghton Mifflin, 1993. **EASY**
The author describes his cross-cultural upbringing in both America and Japan, and his love for both countries. When he lives in one country, he misses the other country. The author knows that his desire to be in both countries at the same time would be well understood by his grandfather. CALDECOTT MEDAL

The Great Ideas of Lila Fenwick by Kate Hall McMullan. Puffin, 1988. **CHALLENGING**
Lila and her friends join her doctor father at a Boy Scout camp. Humorous stories of their adventures are told.

June Mountain Secret by Nina Kidd. HarperCollins, 1991. **AVERAGE**
Soft watercolors illustrate this lovely story about a little girl and her trip with her father when they go fly-fishing for rainbow trout. OUTSTANDING SCIENCE TRADE BOOK

Kate Heads West by Pat Brisson. Macmillan, 1990. **AVERAGE**
On this trip Kate accompanies her friend Lucy and her family through the American Southwest. Kate's letters to friends and relatives tell about the historic places and natural wonders she has seen. AWARD-WINNING AUTHOR

Making Friends by Margaret Mahy. Macmillan, 1990. **AVERAGE**
Their destiny is assured when lonely Mrs. de Vere and lonely Mr. Derry separately adopt clever dogs from the pound. When the friends from the pound meet again on a walk, they make sure that their owners' lives change forever.

Snowshoe Thompson by Nancy Smiler Levinson. HarperCollins, 1992. **EASY**
A letter had to be delivered, so John Thompson traveled ninety miles to carry it across the Sierra Nevada mountains. This feat earned him the nickname Snowshoe Thompson. NOTABLE CHILDREN'S TRADE BOOK IN SOCIAL STUDIES

Tree of Cranes by Allen Say. Houghton Mifflin, 1991. **AVERAGE**
This beautifully illustrated book shows two cultures blending in love and peace as a young Japanese boy has his first Christmas with his American-born mother. ALA NOTABLE BOOK

Daily Language Practice

A PLACE TO DREAM

Language Skills

UNIT ONE
Being Special

THEME: Planting a Seed — Capitalization and punctuation of different kinds of sentences; word order; spelling; correction of sentence fragments (no subject)

THEME: Being Different — Correction of sentence fragments (no predicate); spelling; review of sentence fragments (no subject) and capitalization and punctuation of different kinds of sentences

THEME: Listen to This! — Combining two sentences that have the same subject or the same predicate; capitalization of proper nouns; common nouns in lowercase; spelling; avoidance of run-on sentences

UNIT TWO
Friendships

THEME: School Days — Correct forms for singular and plural nouns *(s, es);* spelling; review of capitalization of proper nouns

THEME: Caring and Sharing — Correct forms of irregular nouns; correct punctuation of singular possessive nouns; spelling; review of correct forms of singular and plural nouns *(s, es)*

THEME: Learning About Yourself — Correct punctuation of plural possessive nouns; spelling; review of punctuation of singular possessive nouns and capitalization of proper nouns

UNIT THREE
Adventures

THEME: Picture This! — Capitalization of the pronoun *I;* correct use of subject pronouns; spelling; review of punctuation of plural possessive nouns

THEME: Mysteries to Solve — Correct use of object pronouns; spelling; review of subject pronouns

THEME: The Great Outdoors — Positive form of adjectives *(how many, what kind)*; spelling; review of subject and object pronouns

SEA OF WONDER

Language Skills

UNIT ONE
Creatures

THEME: Following Animal Friends — Correct use of articles; correct forms of comparison with adjectives; correct use of action verbs; spelling; review of adjectives in the positive form *(how many, what kind)*

THEME: Flights of Fancy — Correct use of main and helping verbs; spelling; review of correct use of action verbs

THEME: Unusual Pets — Keeping tenses consistent; correct use of present-time verbs; spelling; review of correct use of main and helping verbs

UNIT TWO
Puzzlers

THEME: Whether the Weather — Correct use of regular and irregular past-time verbs; spelling; review of correct use of present-time verbs

THEME: Being Clever — Correct use of more irregular present- and past-time verbs; spelling

THEME: Using Your Wits — Subject-verb agreement; correct use of the verb *be;* spelling; review of correct use of irregular verbs

UNIT THREE
Memories

THEME: Remembering — Correct use of adverbs; correct use of troublesome words (homophones) *to* and *your;* spelling; review of subject-verb agreement and correct use of the verb *be*

THEME: Treasures from the Past — Correct use of troublesome words (homophones) *its, their;* spelling; review of troublesome words (homophones) *to, your;* review of correct use of adverbs

THEME: Was It Real? — Comma usage: series, in introductory words; spelling; review of troublesome words (homophones) *to, your, its, their*

SENTENCES OF THE DAY

❶

❷

PROOFREADER'S MARKS

≡ Capitalize.

⊙ Add a period.

∧ Add a comma.

⌄⌄ Add quotation marks.

⁊ Cut something.

⌒ Replace something.

∽ Trade places.

◯ Spell correctly.

¶ Indent paragraph.

/ Make a lowercase letter.

UNIT 1

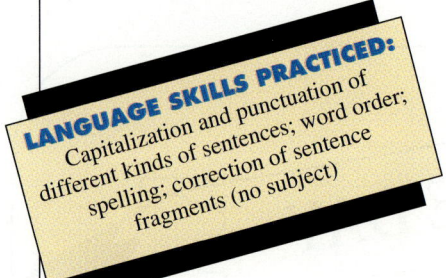

LANGUAGE SKILLS PRACTICED: Capitalization and punctuation of different kinds of sentences; word order; spelling; correction of sentence fragments (no subject)

Being Special

THEME: Planting a Seed

---

1. i saw a man do a curious ack
2. did he take seeds from the pack on his bak

· ·

1. I saw a man do a curious act.
2. Did he take seeds from the pack on his back?

---

7. do you like to look at the figureheads on ships
8. the hed on this one reminds me of my sister

· ·

7. Do you like to look at the figureheads on ships?
8. The head on this one reminds me of my sister!

---

3. look at that man
4. he is throwing bred to the birds

· ·

3. Look at that man!
4. He is throwing bread to the birds.

---

9. i get great satisfaction from planting seeds
10. shall we reast before we plant more?

· ·

9. I get great satisfaction from planting seeds.
10. Shall we rest before we plant more?

---

5. is she planting lupine seeds by haend
6. the wind blew away her het?

· ·

5. Is she planting lupine seeds by hand?
6. The wind blew away her hat!

---

11. what fun it woud be to walk in the wilderness!
12. Let's form a clob and pretend we are pioneers.

· ·

11. What fun it would be to walk in the wilderness!
12. Let's form a club and pretend we are pioneers.

Unit vocabulary is underlined. Spelling words are printed in red.

13. plant pear trees we will for the first settlers
14. we can hunte and fish for our food.

- - -

13. We will plant pear trees for the first <u>settlers</u>.
14. <u>We</u> can hunt and fish for our food.

15. have you ever seen a pear orchard
16. we pick pears from manny orchards

- - -

15. Have you ever seen a pear <u>orchard</u>?
16. We pick pears from many <u>orchards</u>.

17. Ever seen sech beautiful apples? These apples are called Granny Smiths. wonder how they got that name?

- - -

17. Have you ever seen such beautiful apples? These apples are called Granny Smiths. Do you wonder how they got that name?

18. my father talked about different kinds of apples in his recollections. I thinck many are grown in washington. Are not red. they are golden yellow.

- - -

18. My father talked about different kinds of apples in his <u>recollections</u>. I think many are grown in Washington. They are not red. They are golden yellow.

19. My brother is taking the apples to town in the trucke. he thinks the sweet taste of the apples is greatly exaggerated. Likes the tart ones.

- - -

19. My brother is taking the apples to town in the truck. He thinks the sweet taste of the apples is greatly <u>exaggerated</u>. He likes the tart ones.

20. what kind of fruit tree do you like best! i like orange treees. the oranges are so juicy!

- - -

20. What kind of fruit tree do you like best? I like orange trees. The oranges are so juicy!

A PLACE TO DREAM

UNIT 1

Being Special
THEME: Being Different

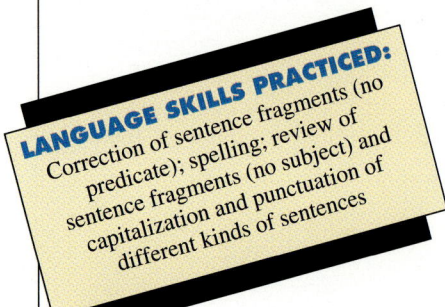
LANGUAGE SKILLS PRACTICED: Correction of sentence fragments (no predicate); spelling; review of sentence fragments (no subject) and capitalization and punctuation of different kinds of sentences

---

1. Thought I would dye when I saw that silly movey!
2. do not like adventures like thiiis one!

---

1. I thought I would **die** when I saw that silly movie!
2. I do not like <u>adventures</u> like this one!

---

3. In the movie, a gray monster took flite.
4. I Saw that the monster was just a cat with a huge shado!

---

3. In the movie, a gray monster took **flight**.
4. I saw that the monster was just a cat with a huge shadow!

---

5. What a frite i received!
6. Like to be assigned a job that is not so scary.

---

5. What a **fright** I received!
6. I'd like to be <u>assigned</u> a job that is not so scary.

---

7. Our first gole.
8. The thief that hid the money

---

7. Our first **goal** is (to catch the thief).
8. The thief that hid the money (is here).
   or
   The thief hid the money.

---

9. The gote that was lost.
10. its nickname.

---

9. The **goat** that was lost (has been found).
   or
   The **goat** was lost.
10. Its <u>nickname</u> (is Clown).

---

11. being different from others.
12. Children in my music clas

---

11. Being different from others (can be fun).
12. Children in my music class (have good times).

Unit vocabulary is underlined. Spelling words are printed in red.

13. let's lye in wait for the door to opin.
14. how exciting it is to solve cases

- -

13. Let's lie in wait for the door to open.
14. How exciting it is to solve cases!

15. how can we have adventures in this deep snoe
16. we will have to find them in the apartment

- -

15. How can we have adventures in this deep snow?
16. We will have to find them in the apartment.

17. let's explore the attic? Look out for that box It is about to fal

- -

17. Let's explore the attic. Look out for that box! It is about to fall!

18. how dirty hour hands are? We will need lots of sope to get them clean. where is the towel.

- -

18. How dirty our hands are! We will need lots of soap to get them clean. Where is the towel?

19. What should we do next. I'm tired of reading comic books. let's do somethin exciting

- -

19. What should we do next? I'm tired of reading comic books. Let's do something exciting.

20. Why don't we play in the snow. We can throe snowballs. we may even want to build a snoman.

- -

20. Why don't we play in the snow? We can throw snowballs. We may even want to build a snowman.

A PLACE TO DREAM

UNIT 1

Being Special

THEME: Listen to This!

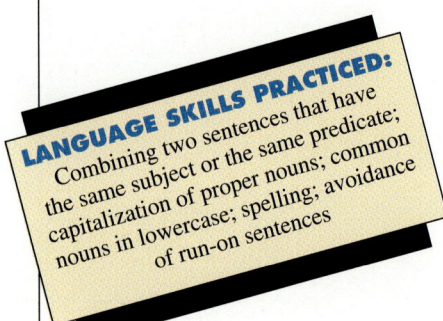

LANGUAGE SKILLS PRACTICED: Combining two sentences that have the same subject or the same predicate; capitalization of proper nouns; common nouns in lowercase; spelling; avoidance of run-on sentences

1. Marie plays the flute. Marie plays the oboe.
2. Tommy plays the drum. Tommy keeps the beet.

- -

1. Marie plays the flute and the oboe.
2. Tommy plays the drum and keeps the beat.

3. Do you play in the orchestra? Does john play in the orchestra?
4. Ron keeps his trumpet clene. I keep my trumpet cleen.

- -

3. Do you and John play in the orchestra?
4. Ron and I keep our trumpets clean.

5. Sara plays instruments. Paul plays instruments.
6. They play on the mane streets of town. They play in the country.

- -

5. Sara and Paul play instruments.
6. They play on the main streets of town and in the country.

7. You want to mete the bassoon player. I want to mete the bassoon player.
8. The bassoon player is a good musician. The flute player is a good musician.

- -

7. You and I want to meet the bassoon player.
8. The bassoon player and the flute player are good musicians.

9. Mr. howell pade us to play for a party.
10. The shrill Notes of my piccolo hurt anna's ears.

- -

9. Mr. Howell paid us to play for a party.
10. The shrill notes of my piccolo hurt Anna's ears.

11. Raze the Cymbals high when you bring them together.
12. The Crash of cymbals makes me think of the rocky mountains.

- -

11. Raise the cymbals high when you bring them together.
12. The crash of cymbals makes me think of the Rocky Mountains.

Unit vocabulary is underlined. Spelling words are printed in red.

13. Wendy and sue play the piano to raise money for a biik.
14. They played for the town of river springs last Week.

---

13. Wendy and Sue play the piano to raise money for a *bike*.
14. They played for the town of River Springs last week.

15. My Parents droove to the city last night.
16. They went to hear the Music on theiir anniversary.

---

15. My parents *drove* to the city last night.
16. They went to hear the music on their *anniversary*.

17. We had tea in a Garden. Musicians played fin music while we ate didn't you love the music?

---

17. We had tea in a garden. Musicians played *fine* music while we ate. Didn't you love the music?

18. The garden was almost empty by Noon what time does it close? The Musicians roose and left long ago.

---

18. The garden was almost *empty* by noon. What time does it close? The musicians *rose* and left long ago.

19. I want to learn to play the piano, the harp, and the violin do you know how to play thees Instruments? Will you show me how

---

19. I want to learn to play the piano, the harp, and the violin. Do you know how to play *these* instruments? Will you show me how?

20. It takes years to learn to play an instrument my sister has studied piano for five years she iz very good now.

---

20. It takes years to learn to play an *instrument*. My sister has studied piano for five years. She is very good now.

A PLACE TO DREAM

DAILY LANGUAGE PRACTICE / R63

UNIT 2

Friendships
THEME: School Days

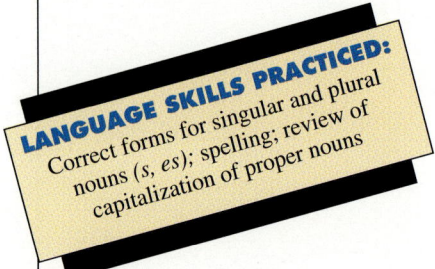

LANGUAGE SKILLS PRACTICED: Correct forms for singular and plural nouns (s, es); spelling; review of capitalization of proper nouns

---

1. I dropped my paperes and crayones on the floor.
2. When I piked them up, I fell and scraped my nee.

- - -

1. I dropped my papers and crayons on the floor.
2. When I picked them up, I fell and scraped my knee.

---

3. In our class we have to rite some linees for commercials.
4. Do you noe any good thinges to do for commercials?

- - -

3. In our class we have to write some lines for commercials.
4. Do you know any good things to do for commercials?

---

5. ali brought floweres and weedes to show the class.
6. If I had noene, i would have brought seedes.

- - -

5. Ali brought flowers and weeds to show the class.
6. If I had known, I would have brought seeds.

---

7. Sometimes i have to laff when i walk.
8. My shoes make funny soundes!

- - -

7. Sometimes I have to laugh when I walk.
8. My shoes make funny sounds!

---

9. Are you laffing at the squirreles?
10. They look funny with acornes and nutes in their cheekes!

- - -

9. Are you laughing at the squirrels?
10. They look funny with acorns and nuts in their cheeks!

---

11. Listen to the chorus of crickets chirping and froges croaking.
12. I would take them to school, but miss braxton might think they're a nuisance.

- - -

11. Listen to the chorus of crickets chirping and frogs croaking.
12. I would take them to school, but Miss Braxton might think they're a nuisance.

Unit vocabulary is underlined. Spelling words are printed in red.

13. What are the fone numbers of the polic station and the fire departmnt?
14. Mr. eckersly said i should keep the numbers by my telefone.

• •

13. What are the phone numbers of the police station and the fire department?
14. Mr. Eckersly said I should keep the numbers by my telephone.

15. I am going to rite a letter to someone in mexico city.
16. The university of mexico is one of the oldest in the wurld!

• •

15. I am going to write a letter to someone in Mexico City.
16. The University of Mexico is one of the oldest in the world!

17. Sami iz late. She must have made a rong turn at ash street. I hope she is not losst.

• •

17. Sami is late. She must have made a wrong turn at Ash Street. I hope she is not lost.

18. Let's go to central threater. Wee are not supposed to giggle at the costumes! I sometimes dew, though.

• •

18. Let's go to Central Theater. We are not supposed to giggle at the costumes! I sometimes do, though.

19. The boston symphony orchestra gave a performance last night. I rote my report about it. What is your report abowt?

• •

19. The Boston Symphony Orchestra gave a performance last night. I wrote my report about it. What is your report about?

20. Our scool putting on a play. I am memorizing my liines. I play the part of king henry.

• •

20. Our school is putting on a play. I am memorizing my lines. I play the part of King Henry.

A PLACE TO DREAM

UNIT 2

Friendships

THEME: Caring and Sharing

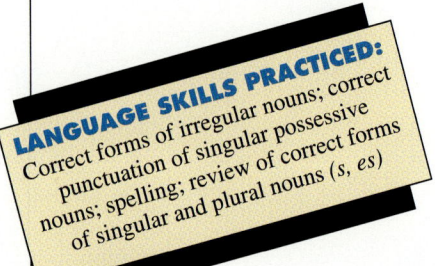

LANGUAGE SKILLS PRACTICED: Correct forms of irregular nouns; correct punctuation of singular possessive nouns; spelling; review of correct forms of singular and plural nouns (s, es)

---

1. Vanna and I must chooze Grandpas birthday presentes.
2. Vanna will get him sockes, but I will get him a klock.

• •

1. Vanna and I must choose Grandpa's birthday presents.
2. Vanna will get him socks, but I will get him a clock.

---

3. Are these fresch berrys on the cake?
4. We must eat the cake promptly so the mouses and antes won't get it!

• •

3. Are these fresh berries on the cake?
4. We must eat the cake promptly so the mice and ants won't get it!

---

5. My mother haz twines, and she lets us take them for walkes.
6. It's raining! You puch the buggyes while I hold the umbrellaes.

• •

5. My mother has twins, and she lets us take them for walks.
6. It's raining! You push the buggies while I hold the umbrellas.

---

7. I help my parentes shop for grocerys.
8. It was stranj to see so many other childs in the store today.

• •

7. I help my parents shop for groceries.
8. It was strange to see so many other children in the store today.

---

9. I learned Braille so I could read storys in my youngest brothers bookes.
10. I have shtrong muscles from imitating my father.

• •

9. I learned Braille so I could read stories in my youngest brother's books.
10. I have strong muscles from imitating my father.

---

11. I ahlmost have enough money to buy Tía Elenas present.
12. I will buy the stores prettiest lace for her dresses collar.

• •

11. I almost have enough money to buy Tía Elena's present.
12. I will buy the store's prettiest lace for her dress's collar.

Unit vocabulary is underlined. Spelling words are printed in red.

13. My mother ahlways buys goats milk.
14. She thinks it is better for her than cows milk or sheeps milk.

- - - - - - - - - - - - - - - - - - - -

13. My mother always buys goat's milk.
14. She thinks it is better for her than cow's milk or sheep's milk.

15. My one brothers plan is to drauw a picture of the house.
16. We wil leave the drawing on Toms desk as a gift.

- - - - - - - - - - - - - - - - - - - -

15. My one brother's plan is to draw a picture of the house.
16. We will leave the drawing on Tom's desk as a gift.

17. This puppies tag says "Ringer." The owners phone number is there, too. I will cal her in case the puppy is lahst.

- - - - - - - - - - - - - - - - - - - -

17. This puppy's tag says "Ringer." The owner's phone number is there, too. I will call her in case the puppy is lost

18. I am glad I caled. The small puppy was Ritas birthday present. She is coming to gett it.

- - - - - - - - - - - - - - - - - - - -

18. I am glad I called. The small puppy was Rita's birthday present. She is coming to get it.

19. Ritas mothers car pulled up. Ringer wentt bounding down the steps to meet Rita. Rita patted Ringers sahft head.

- - - - - - - - - - - - - - - - - - - -

19. Rita's mother's car pulled up. Ringer went bounding down the steps to meet Rita. Rita patted Ringer's soft head.

20. I want to sing a sahng for Elena. Do you know the songs words? I do knot remember them.

- - - - - - - - - - - - - - - - - - - -

20. I want to sing a song for Elena. Do you know the song's words? I do not remember them.

UNIT 2

Friendships

THEME: Learning About Yourself

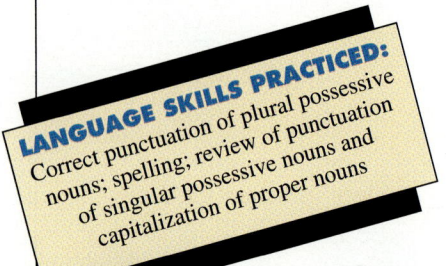

LANGUAGE SKILLS PRACTICED: Correct punctuation of plural possessive nouns; spelling; review of punctuation of singular possessive nouns and capitalization of proper nouns

---

1. I am going to my uncles ranch for New Years Day.
2. We will cuk beans and squash from my aunts garden.

· ·

1. I am going to my uncle's ranch for New Year's Day.
2. We will cook beans and squash from my aunt's garden.

---

3. Uncle Frank loves a cul winters day on the plains.
4. The winds breath is cold, and the suns rays barely warm the prairie.

· ·

3. Uncle Frank loves a cool winter's day on the plains.
4. The wind's breath is cold, and the sun's rays barely warm the prairie.

---

5. While we were cooking outside, my cousins fut got close to the fire.
6. The fires heat almost burned his Toes once.

· ·

5. While we were cooking outside, my cousin's foot got close to the fire.
6. The fire's heat almost burned his toes once.

---

7. My two Uncles use skillets to make the days bread.
8. Each uncles bread is as gude as any you can buy.

· ·

7. My two uncles use skillets to make the day's bread.
8. Each uncle's bread is as good as any you can buy.

---

9. Tonight we will watch the mune and listen to all the trees soft sighs.
10. We will forget the days worries as we rock in Grandpas chairs.

· ·

9. Tonight we will watch the moon and listen to all the trees' soft sighs.
10. We will forget the day's worries as we rock in Grandpa's chairs.

---

11. Tomorrow janna is coming over at nune.
12. We will have a great time mimicking jesse james and Annie oakley.

· ·

11. Tomorrow Janna is coming over at noon.
12. We will have a great time mimicking Jesse James and Annie Oakley.

Unit vocabulary is underlined. Spelling words are printed in red.

13. We will swim in the pule at the san juan Hotel.
14. The hotel is in nearby tempe, arizona.

─────────────────────────────

13. We will swim in the *pool* at the San Juan Hotel.
14. The hotel is in nearby Tempe, Arizona.

15. andre stepped in some mud on rio avenue.
16. Let's stop so andre can scrape his shue.

─────────────────────────────

15. Andre stepped in some mud on Rio Avenue.
16. Let's stop so Andre can scrape his shoe.

17. grandmas supe is the best in the world. She makes it the way the cowboys did in oklahoma. She putts lots of chili in it.

─────────────────────────────

17. Grandma's soup is the best in the world. She makes it the way the cowboys did in Oklahoma. She puts lots of chili in it.

18. Have You ever had chili soup? A cowboy named joe black taught grandma to make it. It iis spicy and good!

─────────────────────────────

18. Have you ever had chili soup? A cowboy named Joe Black taught Grandma to make it. It is spicy and good!

19. mom sayz we can go to the rodeo. We have to split the wude first, though. Mom says our chores have to come furst.

─────────────────────────────

19. Mom says we can go to the rodeo. We have to split the wood first, though. Mom says our chores have to come first.

20. Let's impress Mom and dad. We'll split enough wud for a week. Then maybe they'll let us go to the sand springs rodeo.

─────────────────────────────

20. Let's impress Mom and Dad. We'll split enough wood for a week. Then maybe they'll let us go to the Sand Springs Rodeo.

UNIT 3

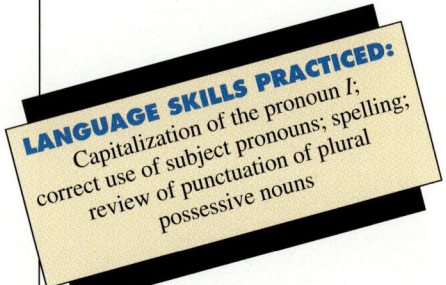

LANGUAGE SKILLS PRACTICED: Capitalization of the pronoun *I*; correct use of subject pronouns; spelling; review of punctuation of plural possessive nouns

Adventures

THEME: Picture This!

---

1. Today i painted a broun river.
2. Many peeple tell me i have a gift for painting, but i don't believe them.

· ·

1. Today I painted a <u>brown</u> river.
2. Many people tell me I have a <u>gift</u> for painting, but I don't believe them.

---

3. My freinds say i should paint a clowd.
4. i would rather doo great deeds.

· ·

3. My friends say I should paint a <u>cloud</u>.
4. I would rather do great <u>deeds</u>.

---

5. i admit that i am proud of my father.
6. i enjoy watching him paint.

· ·

5. I admit that I am proud of my father.
6. I <u>enjoy</u> watching him paint.

---

7. Him is making an oil painting of warriors.
8. Us sometimes uze soyl in our paints.

· ·

7. He is making an <u>oil</u> painting of <u>warriors</u>.
8. We sometimes use <u>soil</u> in our paints.

---

9. Her lives in the toun down the road.
10. Me can see her hous from here.

· ·

9. She lives in the <u>town</u> down the road.
10. I can see her house from here.

---

11. Do your like marmalade as much as i do?
12. i like to eat marmalade and toast in the fresh morning ayre.

· ·

11. Do you like <u>marmalade</u> as much as I do?
12. I like to eat marmalade and toast in the fresh morning <u>air</u>.

Unit vocabulary is underlined. Spelling words are printed in red.

13. Her and him do not want to visit us.
14. Do your think they are afraid of a bair?

---

13. She and he do not want to visit us.
14. Do you think they are afraid of a bear?

---

15. Your may borrow my easel if me may sit in your chare.
16. All the paintings worth will go up when i frame them.

---

15. You may borrow my easel if I may sit in your chair.
16. All the paintings' worth will go up when I frame them.

---

17. The companys gaurd comes every few minutes. Him is a retired police officer. He keeps the paintings saf at night.

---

17. The company's guard comes every few minutes. He is a retired police officer. He keeps the paintings safe at night.

---

18. I am painting a laurge picture. I will enter it in the exhibition. Me am sure it will win a priz.

---

18. I am painting a large picture. I will enter it in the exhibition. I am sure it will win a prize.

---

19. The paintings in this stor are antiques. Most of them are raere. Them are too expensive for me!

---

19. The paintings in this store are antiques. Most of them are rare. They are too expensive for me!

---

20. These paintings owner will be here later. Her also owns the printers shop down the street. She must be the worlds richest person!

---

20. These paintings' owner will be here later. She also owns the printer's shop down the street. She must be the world's richest person!

UNIT 3

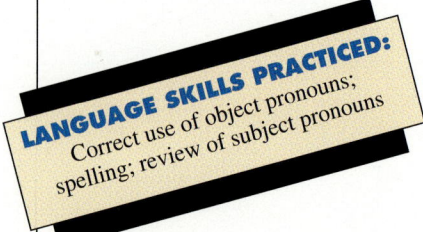

LANGUAGE SKILLS PRACTICED: Correct use of object pronouns; spelling; review of subject pronouns

Adventures

THEME: Mysteries to Solve

---

1. If my sisters don't behave, Mom won't take we to the picnic.
2. The butler will fource they to behave.

- -

1. If my sisters don't behave, Mom won't take us to the picnic.
2. The <u>butler</u> will force them to behave.

---

3. We will surprise Willa on she forth birthday.
4. Ms. Rai will help we get she to the farm.

- -

3. We will surprise Willa on her fourth birthday.
4. Ms. Rai will help us get her to the farm.

---

5. We will ride hourses when us get there.
6. The horses will take we to the nourth side of the pond.

- -

5. We will ride horses when we get there.
6. The horses will take us to the north side of the pond.

---

7. Me am stumped about what to get she for her birthday.
8. Maybe I'll get she scoure cards for her new board game.

- -

7. I am <u>stumped</u> about what to get her for her <u>birthday</u>.
8. Maybe I'll get her score cards for her new board game.

---

9. Us'll have the picnic on the lake's shoure.
10. Ginny will plann it because her's the eldest.

- -

9. We'll have the picnic on the lake's shore.
10. Ginny will plan it because she's the <u>eldest</u>.

---

11. What kind of spourt do them like to play?
12. Let's surprise they and plan lots of outdor sports.

- -

11. What kind of sport do they like to play?
12. Let's surprise them and plan lots of outdoor sports.

Unit vocabulary is underlined. Spelling words are printed in red.

13. What can us do if a stourm comes up?
14. Maybe they will let uz lite the chandelier.

• •

13. What can we do if a storm comes up?
14. Maybe they will let us light the chandelier.

15. Sheila is asking I if us will need sweaters.
16. No, me think it will be very warrm.

• •

15. Sheila is asking me if we will need sweaters.
16. No, I think it will be very warm.

17. I woure sandals on purpose. Me want to be able to take they off. I like to run barefoot in th cool grass.

• •

17. I wore sandals on purpose. I want to be able to take them off. I like to run barefoot in the cool grass.

18. Who will bring the food? I think a professional cook is bringing its. Youse will have many good things to eat.

• •

18. Who will bring the food? I think a professional cook is bringing it. You will have many good things to eat.

19. Is youre father going to the picnic with we? I hope so. Him alwayz has good stories to tell.

• •

19. Is your father going to the picnic with us? I hope so. He always has good stories to tell.

20. Oh, no! Me ripped my sleeve. It's a good thing Rick is hear. Him always carries a needle and thread.

• •

20. Oh, no! I ripped my sleeve. It's a good thing Rick is here. He always carries a needle and thread.

UNIT 3

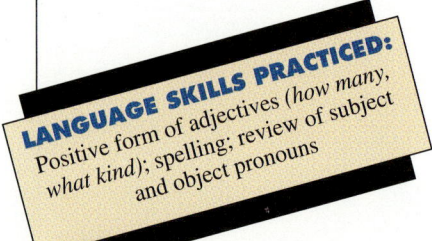

LANGUAGE SKILLS PRACTICED:
Positive form of adjectives (how many, what kind); spelling; review of subject and object pronouns

Adventures

THEME: **The Great Outdoors**

---

1. Can your hear the berd in that tal tree?
2. Its is singing a song to we!

---

1. Can you hear the bird in that tall tree?
2. It is singing a song to us!

---

3. This trail will lead we to a cherch.
4. Its is not well marked, so us might need a compass.

---

3. This trail will lead us to a church.
4. It is not well marked, so we might need a compass.

---

5. If us hike much farther, us will reach the desurt!
6. Don't your like walking with we through the cool forest?

---

5. If we hike much farther, we will reach the desert!
6. Don't you like walking with us through the cool forest?

---

7. The furst night, us camped by a small stream.
8. It rained, so me was glad to have a poncho to keep I dry.

---

7. The first night, we camped by a small stream.
8. It rained, so I was glad to have a poncho to keep me dry.

---

9. My sister brought hur sleeping bag to keep she warm.
10. Dad said me needed to bring one, too, and me did.

---

9. My sister brought her sleeping bag to keep her warm.
10. Dad said I needed to bring one, too, and I did.

---

11. On the first day, Dad fell and almost hert he's knee on a rock.
12. On the thurd day, us went canoeing.

---

11. On the first day, Dad fell and almost hurt his knee on a rock.
12. On the third day, we went canoeing.

Unit vocabulary is underlined. Spelling words are printed in red.

13. Us caught thre fish at camp!
14. it was my tern to tell the good newz.

- - -

13. We caught three fish at camp!
14. It was my turn to tell the good news.

15. Me am sorry I was grumpy with Tina.
16. Her's the onli girl I know who is that nice.

- - -

15. I am sorry I was grumpy with Tina.
16. She's the only girl I know who is that nice.

17. Soon the sun set over the mountins. Us didn't speak a wurd. Not every child gets to see something that beautful.

- - -

17. Soon the sun set over the mountains. We didn't speak a word. Not every child gets to see something that beautiful.

18. us have only tow days left to camp. I do not want to waste the dayz. I want to use they to have more adventures.

- - -

18. We have only two days left to camp. I do not want to waste the days. I want to use them to have more adventures.

19. Sometimes camping is hard wurk. Us hav to gather wood for the campfire. It takes for sticks of wood to start a fire.

- - -

19. Sometimes camping is hard work. We have to gather wood for the campfire. It takes four sticks of wood to start a fire.

20. After the camping trip, my sat at my desk. I wrote down all the fun things that happend. Not meny campers had as much fun as I did this sumer!

- - -

20. After the camping trip, I sat at my desk. I wrote down all the fun things that happened. Not many campers had as much fun as I did this summer!

A PLACE TO DREAM

RESPONSE CARD 1

CHARACTERS

DURING READING

1. Who are the main characters? Who are the minor characters?
2. Do you like or dislike the characters? Why?
3. Does a character in this story remind you of anyone else you have read about? If so, how are they alike?

AFTER READING

4. Choose one character. Why was this character important in the story?
5. Did any of the characters change? If so, how?
6. If you could be any character in this story, who would you be? Why?
7. Suppose you had a chance to meet one of the characters. What would you say to him or her?

Harcourt Brace School Publishers

A PLACE TO DREAM RESPONSE CARDS / R79

RESPONSE CARD 2

SETTING

DURING READING

1. Where does the story take place?
2. Describe the place.
3. Have you ever been to a place like this? If you have, how was it like the place in the story?
4. When does this story take place—long ago, in the future, or in the present? How do you know?

AFTER READING

5. How did the place affect what happened in the story?
6. How would the story be different if it were set in a different place?
7. How would the story be different if it were set in a different time?
8. If you could visit the place, would you go? Why or why not?

Harcourt Brace School Publishers

RESPONSE CARD 3

PLOT

DURING READING

1. Tell the main things that have happened so far.
2. What is the problem in the story? How do you think it will be solved?
3. What do you think will happen next? What do you think will happen at the end?

AFTER READING

4. Tell the main events that happened in the story.
5. What was the solution to the story problem?
6. Did you guess the ending? How else might the author have ended the story?
7. What do you think was the best part of the story? Why?

Harcourt Brace School Publishers

A PLACE TO DREAM

RESPONSE CARD 4

Theme/Mood

During Reading

1. What do you think the author's message will be? Why do you think that?
2. From the title of the story, what do you think this story will be about?
3. How do you feel at this point in the story? Why?
4. What do you remember most about the story so far?

After Reading

5. What was the author's message? Which story events helped you figure out the message?
6. If you wanted to suggest this story to a friend, what would you say it is mostly about?
7. How do you feel now that you have finished the story? Why?
8. What part was
   - the funniest?
   - the saddest?
   - the most exciting?

Harcourt Brace School Publishers

RESPONSE CARD 5

Author's Viewpoint

During Reading

1. What do you know about the author?
2. What is the author trying to tell you? How do you know?
3. Can you tell what kinds of things (people, places, behavior, feelings) the author likes? If so, how do you know?

After Reading

4. Do you agree with the author? Why or why not?
5. What did the author have to know in order to write this article or story?
6. What else could the author have said to support his or her opinion?

Harcourt Brace School Publishers

RESPONSE CARD 6

Author's Craft

During Reading

1. Have you noticed anything you think the author might bring up again later in the story? If so, what did you notice?
2. Tell about any pictures the author has left in your mind.
3. What words has the author used so far to help you
   - see things in the story?
   - hear things in the story?
   - feel things in the story?
4. What does the dialogue tell you about the characters? Do they talk the way people really talk? Why or why not?

After Reading

5. What is your favorite word, line, or paragraph in the story? Why is it your favorite?
6. What do you like about the way the author has written the story?
7. Would you like to read something else by this author? Why or why not?
8. What was the most important thing you learned from the dialogue in this story?

Harcourt Brace School Publishers

RESPONSE CARD 7

Free Response

During Reading

1. Work with a partner. Look over the story, and decide whether you will read it silently or aloud.
2. Think about the way the story is organized. Decide with your partner how often you will stop to discuss it.
3. Each time you stop, talk about what you have read. Tell what you think, and listen to your partner.
4. Read the next section, and talk about it. Continue doing this until you finish the story.

After Reading

5. Talk about the whole story. Tell what you think, and listen to what your partner says.
   - You might talk about your favorite part of the story.
   - You might discuss the author's writing.
   - You might discuss whether what you thought would happen really did happen.

Harcourt Brace School Publishers

RESPONSE CARD 8

Written Dialogue

During Reading

1. Work with a partner. Silently read the pages your teacher suggests.
2. On a sheet of paper, write a comment about what you read. Then write a question about something you didn't understand.
3. Pass your paper to your partner.
4. Write the answer to your partner's question. Then add a new question to the paper.
5. Pass the paper back to your partner. Answer the new question your partner wrote.

After Reading

6. Read the rest of the story. Repeat steps 2–5.
7. Discuss the story. Use the questions and answers on your paper to help you.

Harcourt Brace School Publishers

RESPONSE CARD 9

Literature Circle

Organizing a Literature Circle

The members of your group

- may want to read the selection independently.
- may want to read the selection together to discuss certain parts during reading.
- should decide how many pages to read and what to discuss.

During and After Reading

Your group members can

- discuss their reactions to part or all of the selection.
- ask questions about parts they did not understand.

Choose a sentence starter to help your group begin a discussion.

1. My first reaction was . . .
2. I loved the way the author . . .
3. I didn't like the part . . .

✏ Writing in Your Personal Journal

Sometimes, the members of your Literature Circle may want to write their responses to the selection and then discuss what each of you has written. Here are some things to write about. Choose one.

1. Think of at least three things that the story reminds you of in another story or in your own lives. Tell about them.
2. Copy in your personal journal an important paragraph, sentence, or word from the selection. Explain why it is important to you.
3. What influenced you most when you read: the setting, one of the characters, or the plot of the story? Write about it.

Harcourt Brace School Publishers

A PLACE TO DREAM RESPONSE CARDS / R87

RESPONSE CARD 10

How Do I Know What I Know?

Before Reading

1. How can I find out what the selection is about?
2. What am I going to be reading to find out?
3. What is the story problem?
4. How is this story problem like problems I have solved?

During Reading

5. What do I know so far?
6. What is the topic or theme of this selection?
7. What questions do I have that are still unanswered?
8. What is the story problem?
9. How do I know what the story problem is?

After Reading

10. Did my first prediction match what happened in the selection?
11. How did I know I should change my predictions?
12. How did I know if the story problem would be resolved?
13. What did the writer do to make me think that?
14. How can I use the information I have learned in everyday life?
15. What else would I still like to know about this topic or theme?

Harcourt Brace School Publishers

ADDITIONAL RESOURCES

The resources on these pages will help you customize your literature–based reading program. They include reproducible masters of writing-form models and handwriting models. Independent Reading Masters and Graphic Organizers are also included.

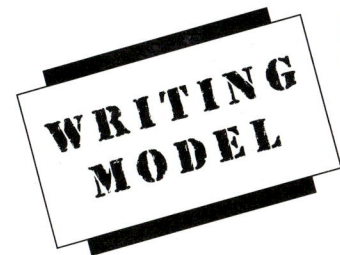

Personal Narrative

*In a **personal narrative,** a writer tells about an experience in his or her life.*

strong beginning

middle that describes events in time order

ending

Why was I named Cameroon Pelée? I never thought about it until a friend asked how I had gotten my name. I didn't know, so I went home to search for answers. First, I sat down to think. Then my sister Helen came in. She was born on the day a volcano named Mount Saint Helens erupted. That's how she got her name. I asked her how I had gotten mine. She said that I got my name the same way she did. It's true. I looked it up. I was born on the same day a volcano erupted in Cameroon, Africa.

Harcourt Brace School Publishers

Paragraph of Information

WRITING MODEL

*A **paragraph of information** gives facts about one topic. It has a topic sentence that tells the main idea. At least two detail sentences give facts about the main idea.*

title

topic sentence

facts

The Peak of Perfection

Mount Cameroon is a special mountain in Africa. It is the highest mountain in western Africa and an active volcano. The last time Mount Cameroon erupted was over 30 years ago. Ash that came out of the volcano turned into rich soil. Farmers now grow tea, rubber trees, and cocoa in that soil. Mount Cameroon is also special because it is one of the wettest places on earth. More than 400 inches of rain fall there each year.

Harcourt Brace School Publishers

Descriptive Paragraph

*A **descriptive paragraph** paints a word picture. It describes a person, a place, an object, or an event.*

topic sentence

detail sentences

words that appeal to the senses (underlined)

    Last fall, the air was <u>crisp</u> and <u>cool</u> as Sam and his big brother waited for the parade to pass. Suddenly, they heard the <u>thump</u> of the <u>big</u> school drum. The parade was coming! Jerry is <u>tall</u>, but even he had trouble seeing over all the people. Beside Jerry a <u>little</u> girl with a <u>sweet-smelling jelly</u> doughnut was crying. She couldn't see a thing. Jerry put her on his shoulders. Then she could see all the <u>high-stepping</u> marchers. The little girl <u>squealed</u> with delight!

Harcourt Brace School Publishers

Story

*In a **story**, a writer tells about one main idea. A story has characters, a plot, and a setting. It also has a beginning, a middle, and an ending.*

title

beginning (characters, setting, problem)

Little Mouse Bells the Cat

The attic mice were all good friends, but they lived in fear of Claws, the house cat. Many mice had damaged tails because of Claws.

"If only we could hear him coming, we'd have time to run away," said Little Mouse.

"We once had a plan to put a bell around his neck," said Bent-Tail.

"That's a great idea," cried Little Mouse. "Why didn't you do it?"

"I bent my tail trying," said Bent-Tail.

Just then, Knotted-Tail ran in. "That cat took my cheese!" he cried.

middle

WRITING MODEL

Suddenly, Little Mouse had an idea. She ran to her nest where she had hidden a bell. She slipped it onto a piece of ribbon. Then she put it on and went downstairs.

Claws heard her coming. "What's making that lovely noise?" he asked.

"It's my wonderful new necklace," squeaked Little Mouse.

"I want it," hissed the cat. "Give it to me, now!"

"Take it!" yelled Little Mouse, as she yanked off the necklace and ran away.

Claws put on his new necklace. He purred when he heard the lovely noise. From that day on, the mice could hear Claws coming.

**ending
(with problem solved)**

Harcourt Brace School Publishers

How-to Paragraph

WRITING MODEL

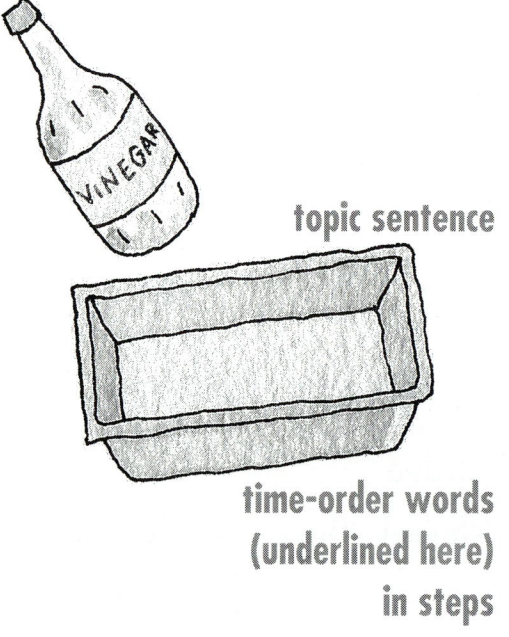

topic sentence

time-order words (underlined here) in steps

*A **how-to paragraph** gives directions or explains how to do something. Steps are given in time order.*

How to Make a Volcano

You can make a small volcano at home with an adult's help. You will need a pan, a plastic bottle, red food coloring, a bottle of vinegar, baking soda, and some sand. <u>First</u>, add a few drops of food coloring to the vinegar. <u>Next</u>, fill the plastic bottle halfway with baking soda and place it in the middle of the pan. Pile the sand around the bottle. <u>Finally</u>, have your adult family member quickly pour the vinegar into the hole. Stand back, and let the volcano erupt.

Harcourt Brace School Publishers

WRITING MODEL

Friendly Letter

*A person writes to someone he or she knows in a **friendly letter.** A friendly letter has five parts: a heading, a greeting, a body, a closing, and a signature. In the heading, the writer includes a comma between the name of the city and state and between the day of the month and the year.*

heading

27 Green Street
Burlington, NC 27215
April 10, 1995

greeting

Dear Grandma,

body

    Sandy and I are fine. Last night he was a busy hamster rearranging the wood shavings in his habitat. I love watching him. Please give Aunt Jenny a hug and a kiss for me.

closing

Love,

signature

Mimi

Harcourt Brace School Publishers

Persuasive Paragraph

*In a **persuasive paragraph**, a writer tries to make readers agree with his or her opinion.*

opinion in topic sentence

reasons and facts

strongest reason last

restated opinion or call for action

Whale-watching is good for people and for the environment. Many people have begun working for earth-friendly causes after sailing near whales. Also, these intelligent animals seem to like the visitors. Tourists describe excitedly how whales come up to the boats to be touched. Most important, whale-watching helps people learn how valuable and beautiful these mysterious mammals are. Everyone is helped by a whale-watching trip. Find out more about one today!

Harcourt Brace School Publishers

Book Review

WRITING MODEL

*A **book review** tells briefly what a book is about without telling the ending. It also gives the writer's opinion of the book. Finally, it says whether others should read it.*

title — Humphrey the Lost Whale

author — The book Humphrey the Lost Whale by Wendy Tokuda and Richard Hall tells the true story of a

main character — young whale that took a wrong turn. In the book, people were at first surprised and pleased to see a whale

setting — in San Francisco Bay. Then Humphrey headed up the Sacramento River. People soon realized he was

main idea of book — lost. Hundreds of people worked together to get Humphrey back to the ocean. This story will make you cheer. Read this book, and share it

whether others should read it — with a friend.

Harcourt Brace School Publishers

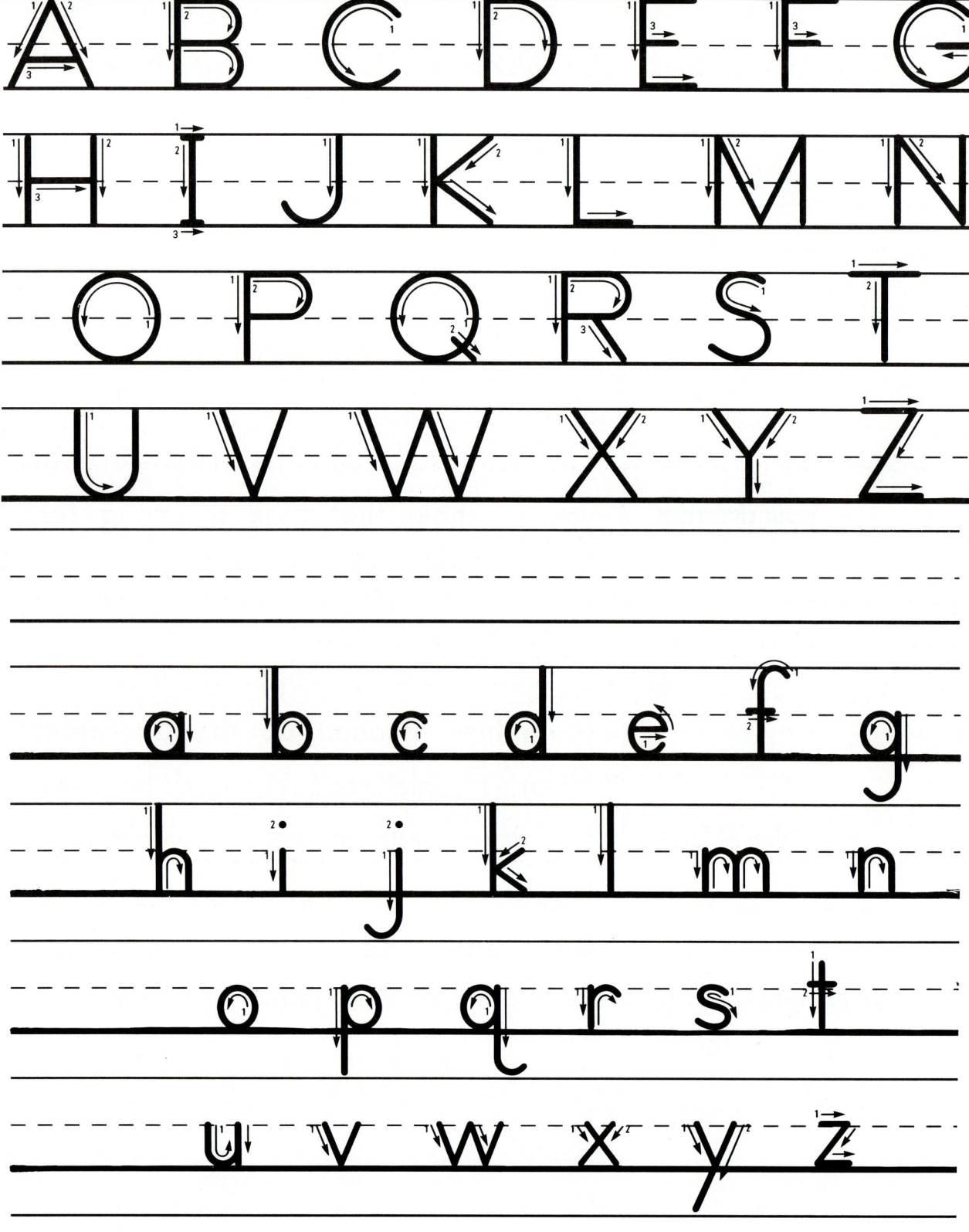

Name _____

Handwriting
Cursive Alphabet

A PLACE TO DREAM

Harcourt Brace School Publishers

REPRODUCIBLE HANDWRITING MODELS / R101

Prediction Chart

What I Predict Will Happen	What Actually Happened

Harcourt Brace School Publishers

Knowledge Chart

Prior Knowledge About _____	New Knowledge About _____
1.	1.
2.	2.
3.	3.
4.	4.
5.	5.
6.	6.
7.	7.

Harcourt Brace School Publishers

Predict-o-Gram

Setting	Characters	Problem	Events	Solution

Harcourt Brace School Publishers

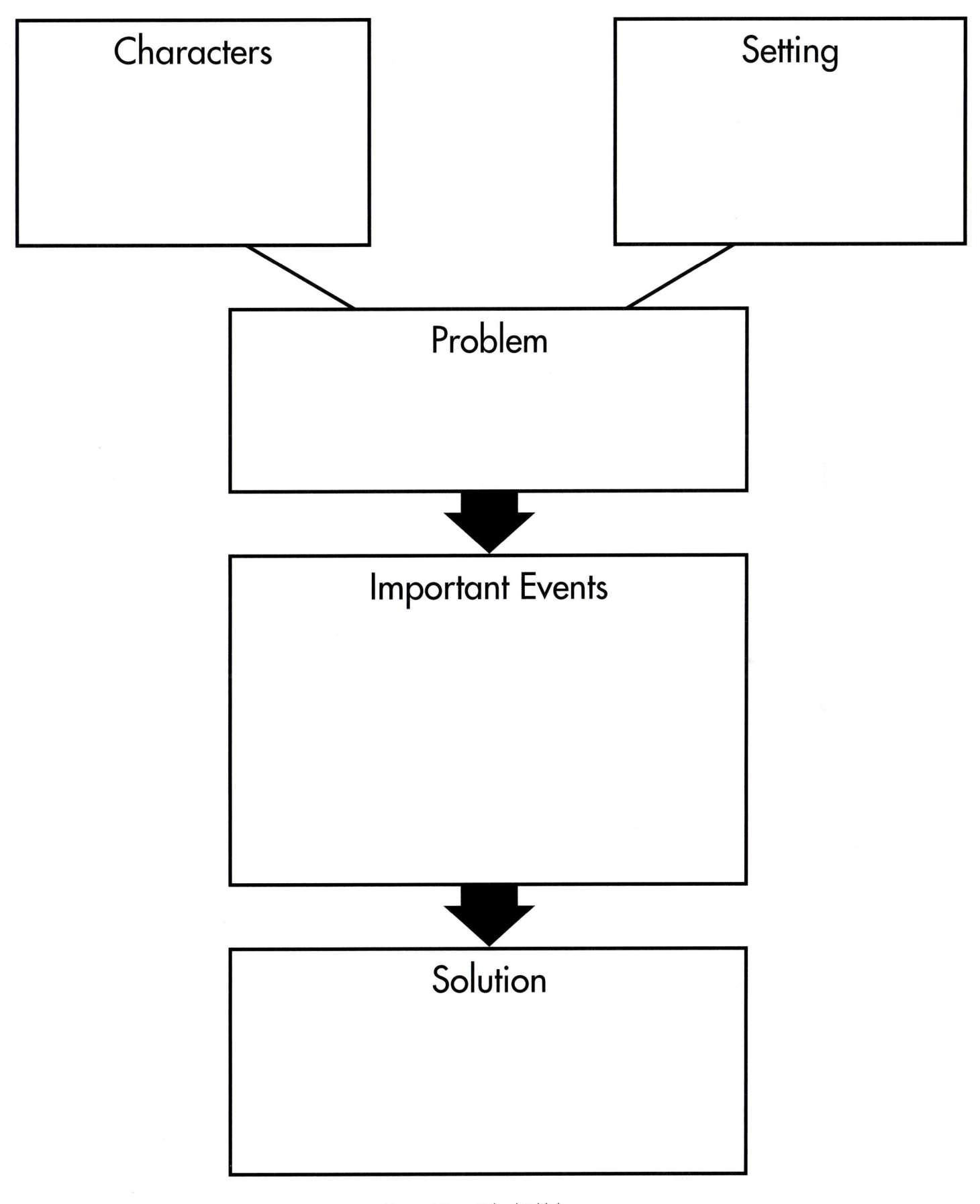

K-W-L Chart

What I Know	What I Want to Know	What I Learned

Harcourt Brace School Publishers

Organizing Ideas

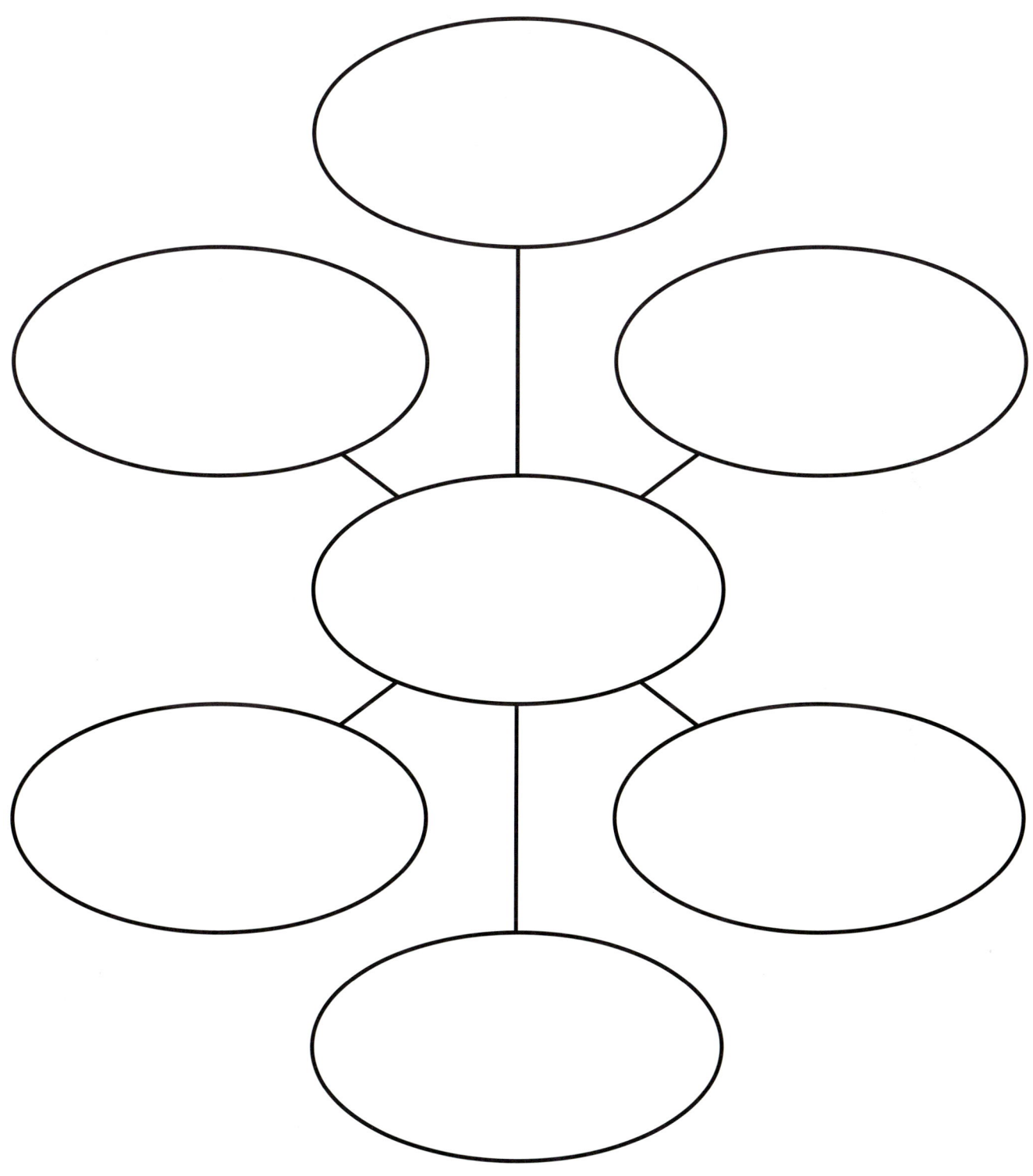

Read All About It

Complete the newspaper page to tell about your book.

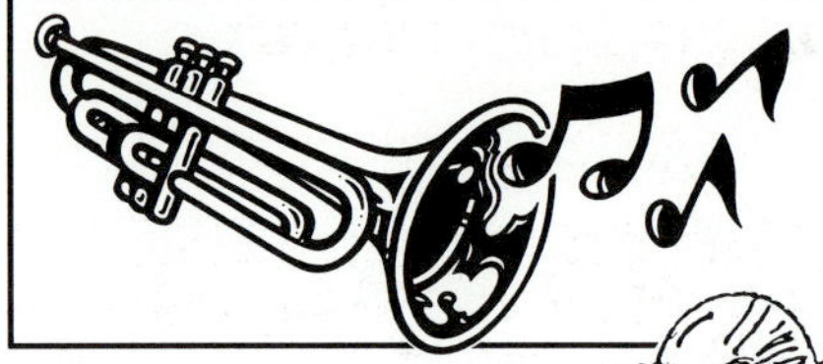

BOOK NOTES
Date: _____

Today's Top Story...

_____ (your name)

Reviews

_____ (book title)

Some of the most interesting things about this book are listed below: _____
_____
_____
_____
_____

Critic's Corner

I thought this book was _____
because _____
_____
_____
_____
_____
_____

A Scene from the Book

This picture shows _____
_____
_____
_____
_____
_____
_____
_____
_____

Harcourt Brace School Publishers

R108 / A PLACE TO DREAM

INDEPENDENT READING MASTERS

Cover to Cover

Name: _____ **Date:** _____

🔍 *Clues from the outside and the inside can help you choose a book.*

Outside

1. Look at the front and back covers of the book you are going to read. Does the book look interesting?

2. Who is the author? Have you read any other books by that author? Did you like them?

Inside

3. Are there any pictures or illustrations? Are the illustrations interesting? Do they make you want to know more about the story?

4. Preview the book. Do you think you will understand and enjoy this book?

What book did you choose? _____

_____

Why did you choose it? _____

_____

Harcourt Brace School Publishers

A PLACE TO DREAM

Think and Decide

Name: _____ **Date:** _____

Write the name of your book. _____

What will you do with your book? Check that box.

☐ Write a letter about your book.

☐ Draw a picture about your book.

☐ Make a puppet.

☐ Act out a scene from your book.

Check one box.

☐ I will work by myself.
☐ I will work with a partner.
☐ I will work in a group.

Make notes here about your plans.

_____
_____
_____

Harcourt Brace School Publishers

R110 / A PLACE TO DREAM

INDEPENDENT READING MASTERS

Notes and Quotes

Name: _____ **Date:** _____

The notepads below may help you keep track of some interesting
or amazing things you'd like to remember from your book.

People/Animals/Characters

Places

Facts or Story Events

New or Interesting Words

yak

Harcourt Brace School Publishers

A PLACE TO DREAM

SCOPE & SEQUENCE AND INDEX

In this section, the Scope and Sequence lists the major objectives of the program. An index and the names of the reviewers who have made contributions to the development of the program are also included.

Treasury of Literature
Scope and Sequence

Grade/Level	K/1	1-1	1-2	1-3	1-4	1-5	2	3	4	5	6	7	8
THINKING													
Observing	M	M	M	M	M	M	M	M	M	M	M	M	M
Brainstorming	M	M	M	M	M	M	M	M	M	M	M	M	M
Classifying and Categorizing	M	M	M	M	M	M	M	M	M	M	M	M	M
Comparing and Contrasting							M	M	M	M	M	M	M
Visualizing	M	M	M	M	M	M	M	M	M	M	M	M	M
Evaluating	M	M	M	M	M	M	M	M	M	M	M	M	M
Synthesizing	M	M	M	M	M	M	M	M	M	M	M	M	M
Analyzing	M	M	M	M	M	M	M	M	M	M	M	M	M
EMERGENT LITERACY													
Phonemic Awareness	M	M	M	M	M	M	M						
Print Awareness	M	M	M	M	M	M	M						
STRATEGIC READING													
Active Reading Strategies	M	M	M	M	M	M	M	M	M	M	M	M	M
Read Fiction (Narrative Text)	M	M	M	M	M	M	M	M	M	M	M	M	M
Read Nonfiction (Expository Text)	M		M	M	M	M	M	M	M	M	M	M	M
Analyze Details	M	M	M	M	M	M	M	M	M	M	M	M	M
Synthesize Ideas/Information	M	M	M	M	M	M	M	M	M	M	M	M	M
Make Inferences	M	M	M	M	M	M	M	M	M	M	M	M	M
Decoding Strategy: Use phonetic/structural analysis plus context to unlock pronunciation	M	M	M	M	M	M	M	M	M	M	M	M	M
Vocabulary Strategy: Use phonetic/structural/contextual clues to determine meanings	M	M	M	M	M	M	M	M	M	M	M	M	M
Use Self-Assessment Strategies	M	M	M	M	M	M	M	M	M	M	M	M	M
COMPREHENSION													
Cause-Effect							♦	♦	♦	♦	♦	♦	♦
Classify/Categorize		♦					♦						
Compare and Contrast								♦	♦	♦	♦	♦	♦
Draw Conclusions					♦		♦	♦	♦	♦	♦	♦	♦
Fact-Fantasy/Nonfact				♦			♦						
Author's Purpose											♦	♦	♦
Author's Viewpoint											♦	♦	♦
Fact-Opinion								♦	♦	♦	♦	♦	♦
Main Idea (Global Meaning)/Details						♦	♦	♦	♦	♦	♦	♦	♦
Make Generalizations											♦	♦	♦
Make Judgments											♦	♦	♦
Paraphrase								♦	♦	♦			
Make Predictions					♦		♦	♦	♦	♦	♦	♦	♦
Referents													
Sequence			♦				♦	♦	♦	♦	♦	♦	♦
Summarize								♦	♦	♦	♦	♦	♦
VOCABULARY													
Key Words/Selection Vocabulary	♦	♦	♦	♦	♦	♦	♦	♦	♦	♦	♦	♦	♦
Synonyms/Antonyms													
Multiple-Meaning Words											♦	♦	♦
Homophones/Homographs													
Context Clues					♦			♦	♦	♦	♦	♦	♦
Vocabulary Strategy: Use phonetic/structural/contextual clues to determine meanings													
Analogies													
Connotation/Denotation													
Glossary													
Dictionary (for Word Meaning)												♦	♦
DECODING													
Phonics													
Initial/Medial/Final Consonants	♦	♦	♦	♦									
Phonograms													
Short Vowels/Long Vowels			♦	♦	♦	♦							
Consonant Clusters/Digraphs (Initial/Final)				♦	♦	♦							
R-Controlled Vowels							♦						

▪ Modeling Instruction/Application   ♦ Tested

Testing options include Unit Reading Skills Assessment, Unit Holistic Reading Assessment, Unit Language and Writing Assessment, and Unit Integrated Performance Assessment.
For a complete scope and sequence of the kindergarten program, see the Teacher's Edition for that level.

Grade/Level	K/1	1–1	1–2	1–3	1–4	1–5	2	3	4	5	6	7	8
Vowel Diphthongs/Vowel Digraphs/Variant Vowels							◆						
Schwa													
Decoding Strategy: Use phonetic/structural analysis plus context to unlock pronunciation	■	■	■	■	■	■	■						
Structural Analysis													
Inflected Forms (Nouns; Verbs With and Without Spelling Changes)		◆	◆		◆		◆						
Possessives, Comparatives, Superlatives													
Contractions				◆	◆								
Compound Words													
Syllabication													
Suffixes/Prefixes								◆	◆	◆	◆	◆	◆
Greek and Latin Roots									◆	◆	◆	◆	◆
Spelling Patterns													

STUDY SKILLS

Locate Sources of Information

	K/1	1–1	1–2	1–3	1–4	1–5	2	3	4	5	6	7	8
Use the Library (Parts of, Card Catalog, Computerized Card Catalog, Call Numbers, Database Searching Strategies, *Books in Print*, *Readers' Guide to Periodical Literature*)													
Alphabet/Alphabetical Order					◆								

Use Sources of Information

	K/1	1–1	1–2	1–3	1–4	1–5	2	3	4	5	6	7	8
Book Parts													
Graphic Aids (Maps, Charts, Graphs, Tables/Schedules, Diagrams, Time Lines)								◆	◆	◆	◆	◆	◆
Compare Information from More Than One Source										◆			◆
Use Reference Sources (Glossary/Dictionary, Thesaurus, Specialized Dictionary, Atlas/Globe, Encyclopedia, Newspaper, *Books in Print*, *Readers' Guide*)									◆	◆	◆	◆	◆
Study Strategies (K-W-L, SQ3R, How to Study)													
Content-Area Reading													
Adjust Method/Rate of Reading													
Test-Taking Strategies													
Outlining/Note-taking Strategies													
Follow Directions			◆				◆	◆	◆	◆	◆	◆	◆
Forms/Applications													

LITERARY APPRECIATION

	K/1	1–1	1–2	1–3	1–4	1–5	2	3	4	5	6	7	8
Select Books for Individual Needs and Interests													
Read Full-length Books													

Literary Elements

	K/1	1–1	1–2	1–3	1–4	1–5	2	3	4	5	6	7	8
Plot Development													
Storyline								◆	◆	◆	◆	◆	◆
Conflict (Internal/External)											◆	◆	◆
Climax													
Flashback/Foreshadowing													
Theme													◆
Character (Emotions, Types, Development, Traits)								◆	◆	◆	◆	◆	◆
Setting								◆	◆	◆	◆	◆	◆
Mood/Tone												◆	◆
Point of View													
Narration													
Dialogue										◆			
Reader Response Groups/Strategies													

Author's Craft/Technique

	K/1	1–1	1–2	1–3	1–4	1–5	2	3	4	5	6	7	8
Figurative Language										◆	◆	◆	◆
Characterization													
Imagery													
Sound Devices (Rhythm/Rhyme/Alliteration/Onomatopoeia)													

Literary Forms/Genre

	K/1	1–1	1–2	1–3	1–4	1–5	2	3	4	5	6	7	8
Fiction													
Realistic Fiction													
Historical Fiction													
Mystery													
Fantasy													
Science Fiction													
Full-length Book													
Riddle													
Drama/Play													

■ Modeling Instruction/Application ◆ Tested

Testing options include Unit Reading Skills Assessment, Unit Holistic Reading Assessment, Unit Language and Writing Assessment, and Unit Integrated Performance Assessment.

For a complete scope and sequence of the kindergarten program, see the Teacher's Edition for that level.

Grade/Level	K/1	1–1	1–2	1–3	1–4	1–5	2	3	4	5	6	7	8
Poetry/Song	■	■	■	■	■	■	■	■	■	■	■	■	■
Nonfiction													
Biography/Autobiography	■	■	■	■	■	■	■	■	■	■	■	■	■
Journal/Diary/Letters							■	■	■	■	■	■	■
Essay									■	■	■	■	■
Informational Article				■	■	■	■	■	■	■	■	■	■
How-to Article					■	■	■	■	■	■	■	■	■
Interview								■	■	■	■	■	■
Speech											■	■	■
Personal Narrative						■	■	■	■	■	■	■	■
Folklore (Folktale, Fairy Tale, Fable, Myth, Tall Tale, Legend, Nursery Rhyme)	■	■	■	■	■	■	■	■	■	■	■	■	■

MULTICULTURALISM

	K/1	1–1	1–2	1–3	1–4	1–5	2	3	4	5	6	7	8
Respond to literature representing our pluralistic culture	■	■	■	■	■	■	■	■	■	■	■	■	■
View concepts/issues from diverse perspectives	■	■	■	■	■	■	■	■	■	■	■	■	■
Understand the concept that all groups have contributed to society	■	■	■	■	■	■	■	■	■	■	■	■	■
Acquire attitudes/skills/knowledge to interact successfully with members of diverse groups	■	■	■	■	■	■	■	■	■	■	■	■	■

LANGUAGE

Composition

	K/1	1–1	1–2	1–3	1–4	1–5	2	3	4	5	6	7	8
Writing Process (Prewriting, Drafting, Revising, Proofreading, Publishing)	■	■	■	■	■	■	■	■	■	■	■	■	■
Writer's Craft													
Capturing Reader's Interest							■	■	■	■	■	■	■
Identifying Audience and Purpose							♦	♦	♦	♦	♦	♦	♦
Using Appropriate Language							♦	♦	♦	♦	♦	♦	♦
Writing Approaches													
Collaborative Writing				■	■	■	■	■	■	■	■	■	■
Shared Writing	■	■	■	■	■	■	■	■	■	■	■	■	■
Timed Writing									■	■	■	■	■
Writing to Prompts							♦	♦	♦	♦	♦	♦	♦
Responding to Essay Questions									■	■	■	■	■
Forms of Writing													
Expository Writing (Comparison/Contrast, Explanation, Directions, Friendly/Business Letters, News Story, Essay, Report)				■	■	■	♦	♦	♦	♦	♦	♦	♦
Narrative Writing (Stories, Paragraphs, Personal Narrative, Personal Journal, Play, Poetry)				■	■	■	♦	♦	♦	♦	♦	♦	♦
Descriptive Writing (Titles, Captions, Paragraphs, Stories, Poetry)				■	■	■	♦	♦	♦	♦	♦	♦	♦
Persuasive Writing (Paragraph/s, Essay, Letter)							♦	♦	♦	♦	♦	♦	♦
Cross-Curricular Writing	■	■	■	■	■	■	■	■	■	■	■	■	■
Everyday Writing (Journals, Messages, Forms, Note Taking, Summaries)	■	■	■	■	■	■	■	■	■	■	■	■	■
Skills of Revision													
Correcting Sentence Fragments/Run-ons							♦	♦	♦	♦	♦	♦	♦
Sentence Combining								♦	♦	♦	♦	♦	♦
Adding/Deleting/Rearranging Information				■	■	■	■	■	■	■	■	■	■
Choosing Words Effectively (Exact/Precise Words, Vivid Words, Trite/Overused Words, Clichés)								♦	♦	♦	♦	♦	♦
Elaborating (Details, Examples, Dialogue, Quotations)				■	■	■	■	♦	♦	♦	♦	♦	♦
Unity and Coherence							♦	♦	♦	♦	♦	♦	♦
Varying Sentence Structure, Word Order, and Sentence Length								♦	♦	♦	♦	♦	♦

Grammar

Sentences

	K/1	1–1	1–2	1–3	1–4	1–5	2	3	4	5	6	7	8
Types (Declarative, Interrogative, Exclamatory, Imperative)		■	■	■	■	■	♦	♦	♦	♦	♦	♦	♦
Structure (Simple, Compound, Complex)								♦	♦	♦	♦	♦	♦
Parts (Subjects/Predicates: Complete, Simple, Compound; Clauses: Independent, Subordinate)				■	■	■	♦	♦	♦	♦	♦	♦	♦
Complements (Direct/Indirect Objects; Predicate Nominatives/Adjectives)											♦	♦	♦
Word Order		■	■	■	■	■	♦	♦					
Nouns (Singular, Plural, Common, Proper, Possessive, Collective, Abstract, Concrete; Abbreviations)				■	■	■	♦	♦	♦	♦	♦	♦	♦
Verbs (Action, Helping, Linking, Transitive, Intransitive, Regular, Irregular)					■	■	♦	♦	♦	♦	♦	♦	♦
Verb Tenses (Present, Past, Future; Present, Past, Future Perfect)							♦	♦	♦	♦	♦	♦	♦
Verbals (Participles, Gerunds, Infinitives)											■	■	■
Adjectives (Common, Proper; Articles)					■	■	♦	♦	♦	♦	♦	♦	♦
Adverbs (Place, Time, Manner, Degree; Negatives)								♦	♦	♦	♦	♦	♦
Pronouns (Subject, Object, Possessive, Reflexive, Demonstrative)							♦	♦	♦	♦	♦	♦	♦

■ Modeling Instruction/Application   ♦ Tested

Testing options include Unit Reading Skills Assessment, Unit Holistic Reading Assessment, Unit Language and Writing Assessment, and Unit Integrated Performance Assessment.
For a complete scope and sequence of the kindergarten program, see the Teacher's Edition for that level.

	Grade/Level	K/1	1–1	1–2	1–3	1–4	1–5	2	3	4	5	6	7	8
Prepositions; Prepositional Phrases											♦	♦	♦	♦
Conjunctions														
Usage														
Nouns (Abbreviations, Plural Forms, Appositives)								♦	♦	♦	♦	♦	♦	♦
Verbs (Subject-Verb Agreement)								♦	♦	♦	♦	♦	♦	♦
Adjectives (Articles; Positive, Comparative, Superlative)								♦	♦	♦	♦	♦	♦	♦
Adverbs (Positive, Comparative, Superlative; Double Negatives)										♦	♦	♦	♦	♦
Pronouns (Antecedents, Subject, Object, Possessive, and Reflexive Forms)										♦	♦	♦	♦	♦
Troublesome Words									♦	♦	♦	♦	♦	♦
Mechanics														
Capitalization (In Sentence, Pronoun I, Proper Nouns and Adjectives, Titles)								♦	♦	♦	♦	♦	♦	♦
Punctuation (Indention, Period, Question Mark, Exclamation Point, Comma, Underlining, Apostrophe, Quotation Marks, Colon, Hyphen, Semicolon, Parentheses, Dash)								♦	♦	♦	♦	♦	♦	♦
Listening														
Participate in Cooperative Groups														
Receive Directions/Gain Information/Enhance Appreciation of Language														
Respond to a speaker by retelling what was heard, asking questions, and/or contributing information														
Analyze/Evaluate Intent and Content of Speaker's Message														
Note Details														
Visualize														
Determine Problem/Solution														
Make Justifiable Inferences														
Identify Supporting Details														
Recognize Persuasion														
Identify Mood/Tone														
Recognize Bias/Prejudice/Propaganda/Emotional Appeals														
Speaking														
Participate in Cooperative Groups														
Identify Audience/Purpose														
Use a Variety of Words to Convey Meaning														
Describe Personal Ideas, Feelings, and Expressions														
Orally Retell/Summarize Stories														
Entertain Others with Stories, Poems, Dramatic Activities														
Give Directions														
Share Information														
Compare/Contrast														
Persuade Others														
Develop Skill in Using the Conventions of English														
Handwriting														
Letter Forms (Manuscript, Cursive)														
Elements														
Common Errors														
Integrated Spelling														
Sound-Letter Relationships (Consonants, Vowels, Schwa, Double Letters, Stress and Accents)														
Word Structure (Plural Nouns/Inflected Verbs and Adjectives With and Without Spelling Changes, Prefixes, Suffixes, Greek and Latin Roots, Abbreviations, Contractions, Possessives, Compound Words)														
Word Analysis (Syllable/Letter Patterns, Pronunciation and Stress, Phonograms, Rhyming Words, Related Words, Word Origins)														
Study Methods and Strategies (Rhyming Words, Pronunciation, Word Shapes, Placeholder, Dictionary, Related Words, Mnemonic Devices, Proofreading)														
Apply Spelling Generalizations					♦	♦	♦	♦	♦	♦	♦	♦	♦	♦
Apply Spelling Strategies														
Master Frequently Misspelled Words														

■ **Modeling Instruction/Application** ♦ **Tested**
Testing options include Unit Reading Skills Assessment, Unit Holistic Reading Assessment, Unit Language and Writing Assessment, and Unit Integrated Performance Assessment.
For a complete scope and sequence of the kindergarten program, see the Teacher's Edition for that level.

INDEX

Active reading strategies, T252
  introduce, T38–39
  review, T75, T271
  reteach, R5
  See also Preview and predict; Purpose for reading/listening; Strategic reading, suggestions for.
Additional reading, T17, T41, T51, T77, T87, T127, T151, T155, T185, T211, T237, T247, T268, T273, T279, T298, T303, T313, T343, T367, T403, T422, T424, T427, T437, T458, T463, T477, T501, R45–52
  See also Bookshelf; Harcourt Brace Library.
Additional resources
  See Resources, additional.
Adjectives
  introduce, T494–495
  test, T513
  reteach, R34
  See also Grammar.
Affixes
  See Structural analysis; Structural and contextual clues; Structural clues.
Alliteration
  See Literary elements and techniques.
Almanac
  See Reference sources.
Alphabetical order
  introduce, T108–109
  reteach, R10
  See also Reference sources.
Analogies
  See Synonyms, antonyms, analogies.
Analyzing details
  See Details.
Antonyms
  See Synonyms, antonyms, analogies.
Apostrophe
  See Mechanics.
Art activities, T6, T33, T39, T40, T41, T42, T48, T64, T67, T71, T76, T77, T105, T112, T113, T114, T138, T141, T149, T150, T179, T184, T187, T189, T201, T229, T236, T244, T272, T273, T274, T297, T302, T303, T304, T343, T345, T351, T398, T419, T426, T428, T454, T462, T464, T493, T501
Assessment options
  formal
    holistic reading assessment, T7, T193, T197, T353, T357, T513
    integrated performance assessment, T7, T193, T197, T353, T357, T513
    reading skills assessment, T7, T193, T197, T353, T357, T513
    writing and language skills assessment, T7, T193, T197, T353, T357, T513
  informal
    informal/performance assessment, T7, T22, T37, T39, T47, T60, T71, T73, T97, T109, T111, T134, T145, T147, T149, T161, T181, T193, T197, T207, T218, T224, T231, T233, T241, T252, T261, T269, T284, T299, T327, T339, T353, T357, T379, T395, T416, T447, T485, T513
    portfolio conference, T7, T193, T197, T353, T357, T513
    reading/writing portfolio, T7, T13, T81, T83, T121, T123, T189, T193, T197, T203, T241, T243, T292, T307, T309, T349, T363, T431, T433, T473, T508, T509
    retelling, oral/written, T7, T193, T197, T357, T513
    running records, T7, T193, T197, T353, T357, T431, T509, T513
    strategy conference, T29, T63, T81, T121, T137, T173, T189, T223, T241, T260, T291, T307, T330, T349, T387, T415, T431, T450, T471, T489, T509
    student self-assessment, T7, T30, T64, T81, T102, T121, T173, T189, T193, T197, T241, T292, T307, T330, T349, T353, T388, T431, T471, T490, T509
    summarizing, T431, T451
  options, T7, T81, T121, T189, T193, T197, T241, T307, T349, T353, T357, T431, T471, T509, T513
Atlas
  See Reference sources.
At-risk students
  See Managing the literature-based classroom; Meeting individual needs.
Audiovisual materials (audio resources, literature cassettes, software, video resources), T6, T196, T356
Auditory modality
  See Modalities of learning, teaching through; Reteach lessons.
Author's craft
  See Literary elements and techniques.
Authors in Teacher's Guide
  Clark, Margaret Goff, T10
  Peters, Lisa Westberg, T200
  Sobol, Donald, T360
Authors of program, iii–v
  Abrahamson, Richard F.
  Church, Ellen Booth
  Coulter, Barbara Bowen
  Cullinan, Bernice E.
  Farr, Roger C.
  Gallego, Margareta
  Hammond, W. Dorsey
  Irvin, Judith L.
  Kupiter, Karen
  Ogle, Donna M.
  Shanahan, Timothy
  Smith, Patricia
  Strickland, Dorothy S.
  Yokota, Junko
  Yopp, Hallie Kay
Authors of selections, discussing
  Bond, Michael, T403
  Bradley, Alfred, T403
  Cleary, Beverly, T205, T211, T221
  Cooney, Barbara, T17, T28, T80
  dePaola, Tomie, T367, T386
  Hayes, Ann, T127
  Hurwitz, Johanna, T87, T100
  Kellogg, Steven, T51
  MacLachlan, Patricia, T247
  Say, Allen, T477, T488
  Taha, Karen, T279
  Walter, Mildred Pitts, T313, T329
  Williams, Vera B., T155, T160, T172
  Yolen, Jane, T437, T449
  See also Poets in Anthology.
Author's purpose
  introduce, T232–233
  review, T270
  reteach, R20
  See also Literary elements and techniques.
Autobiographical story
  See Literary forms.
Autobiographies
  See Reference sources.

Background, building, T10, T18, T43, T44, T45, T52, T59, T88, T128, T156, T200, T205, T212, T248, T257, T275, T280, T282, T314, T326, T360, T368, T375, T377, T378, T404, T408, T409, T410, T438, T465, T478
Base words
  See Structural analysis; Structural and contextual clues; Structural clues.
Biography
  See Literary forms; Reference sources.
Book report/review
  See Literary forms.
Bookshelf, T9, T199, T359
  See also Additional reading; Harcourt Brace Library.
Brainstorming, T33, T71, T101, T120, T149, T150, T174, T188, T194, T212, T226, T236, T239, T240, T263, T306, T345, T348, T370, T416, T454, T493
British English
  See Language, diversities of.
Brochures
  See Reference sources.
Bulletin board ideas, T6, T40, T112, T121, T189, T196, T343, T351, T356, T398, T419, T501

Calendar
  See Reference sources.
Capitalization
  See Mechanics.
Card catalog
  See Reference sources; Sources of information.
Career activities, T236
Catalogs
  See Reference sources.
Categorizing and classifying, T19, T63, T213, T314
Cause and effect
  introduce, T36–37
  review, T74, T183
  test, T193
  reteach, R4
Challenge activities
  See Meeting individual needs.
Character
  See Literary elements and techniques; Story elements.
Characterization
  See Literary elements and techniques.
Charts
  See Graphic organizers.

INDEX / R119

Classifying
See Categorizing and classifying.
Classroom management
See Managing the literature-based classroom.
Collaborative response
See Reader response groups.
Community involvement, T76, T77, T237, T238, T302, T427, T501
Compare and contrast, T40, T47, T58, T115, T137, T188, T189, T207, T239, T260, T424, T429, T445, T466, T469, T503, T507, T513
Compound words, T31, T65, T95, T484
Comprehension/Literature skills
See Author's purpose; Cause and effect; Fiction and nonfiction, distinguishing between; Figurative language; Main idea and details; Plays, elements of; Point of view; Predictions, making; Story elements (plot, setting, characters, dialogue).
Comprehension strategies
See Active reading strategies; Synthesizing ideas.
Computer software
audiovisual materials and software, T6, T196, T356
computer tip, T81, T121, T189, T240, T306, T348, T430, T471, T508
Computerized card catalog
See Reference sources; Sources of information.
Conclusions, drawing, T11, T29, T116, T201, T276, T291, T320, T322, T383, T415, T446, T466, T489, T504
Conflict
See Literary elements and techniques.
Context clues
introduce, T422–423
review, T461, T499
test, T513
reteach, R30
See also Structural and contextual clues.
Contractions
See Mechanics.
Cooperative learning
grammar minilesson, T35, T179
integrated curriculum, T112, T150, T151, T184, T236, T273, T302, T342, T398, T462
integrated language arts, T33, T140, T227, T265, T295, T334, T391, T418, T419, T454, T493, T500
learning through the literature, T39, T71, T73, T77, T111, T145, T147, T149, T231, T299
responding to the selection, T29, T48, T63, T101, T137, T173, T208, T223, T260, T330, T415, T450, T489
See also Critical thinking; Reader response groups.
Cooperative reading
See Reader response groups.
Creative dramatics
See Drama.
Creative thinking, T29, T47, T48, T63, T101, T102, T115, T137, T173, T207, T208, T223, T224, T260, T275, T291, T330, T331, T345, T387, T415, T430, T450, T465, T489, T503
Critical thinking, T29, T30, T47, T48, T63, T64, T101, T102, T137, T138, T173, T194, T207, T208, T223, T224, T260, T261, T291, T292, T330, T331, T387, T388, T415, T416, T429, T450, T451, T489
Cultural awareness, T8, T10, T24, T40, T41, T52, T76, T88, T93, T112, T128, T135, T141, T151, T156, T168, T184, T185, T198, T212, T236, T248, T273, T280, T284, T289, T303, T314, T326, T343, T358, T368, T372, T377, T409, T410, T426, T464, T478, T501
See also Multicultural Connections; Multicultural Perspectives.
Curriculum connections
See Integrated curriculum.

Daily Language Practice
blackline master, R57
introduction, R53
proofreading marks, R57
sentences, R58–75
skills matrix, R55–56
Dance, T400
Decoding strategies
See Structural analysis; Structural and contextual clues; Structural clues.
See also Vocabulary strategies.
Description
See Literary elements and techniques.
Descriptive paragraph
See Literary forms.
Details, analyzing, T361, T415
See also Main idea and details.
Diagrams
See Graphic organizers.
Dialogue
See Literary elements and techniques.
Dialogue, punctuating
See Mechanics.
Dictionary
See Reference sources.
Directions, following
introduce, T70–71
review, T182, T301
test, T193
reteach, R7
Drafting
See Process writing steps; Writer's Workshop.
Drama, T11, T14, T30, T32, T107, T176, T224, T226, T263, T292, T294, T333, T344, T393, T418, T419, T424–425, T453, T490, T492, T497, T503
Drawing conclusions
See Conclusions.

Encyclopedia
See Reference sources.
Ending
See Literary elements and techniques.
Events
See Literary elements and techniques.
Extending vocabulary
See Vocabulary, extending.
Extra help
See Meeting individual needs; Reteach lessons; Second-language support.

Family involvement, T6, T16, T50, T67, T77, T86, T126, T154, T179, T196, T210, T246, T278, T312, T335, T356, T366, T402, T436, T476, T493
Fantasy
See Literary forms.
Fantasy and reality, distinguishing between
See Literary elements and techniques.
Fiction
See Literary forms.
Fiction and nonfiction, distinguishing between
introduce, T458–459
reteach, R33
Figurative language (idiom, metaphor, simile)
introduce, T338–339
reteach, R26
See also Literary elements and techniques.
Fluency, oral reading
See Oral rereading; Speaking, oral report/presentation; Speaking and oral reading, guidelines for.
Following directions
See Directions, following.
Foreign languages, words from
See Language, diversities of.
Formal assessment
See Assessment options, formal.
Fragments
See Grammar.

Generalizations, making, T23
Genres
See Literary forms.
Gifted and talented students
See Meeting individual needs.
Globe, using
See Reference sources.
Glossary
introducing, T515
See also Reference sources.
Grammar
adjectives, T494–495, R34, R74–75
combining, T509
placement of, in English, T434
nouns
common, T142–143, T164, T176, T189, T226, R12, R62–63
exact, T188, T189
irregular, T266–267, T294, R21, R66–67
plural, T228–229, T258, T263, T266–267, T287, T294, T307, R18, R21, R64–65, R66–67
possessive (singular and plural), T296–297, T318, T333, T336–337, T349, T384, T390, R23, R25, R66–67, R68–69, R70–71
proper, T19, T53, T178–179, T189, T213, T219, T226, T241, T431, T439, R16, R62–63, R64–65, R68–69
singular, T228–229, T258, T263, T266–267, R18, R64–65, R66–67
predicates
simple, compound, complete, T121, R62–63
subject and, T106–107, T121, T132, T140, R6, R9, R60–61
pronouns
object, T456–457, T485, T492, T509, R32, R72–73, R74–75
singular and plural, T392–393, T412, T418, R27, R70–71
subject, T420–421, T431, T447, T453, T471, T509, R29, R70–71, R72–73, R74–75
sentences
defined, T23, T32, T34–35, T140, R3
fragment, T81, T132, R58–59, R60–61
kinds of (declarative, exclamatory, imperative, interrogative), T23, T32, T34–35, T61, T66, R3, R58–59, R60–61

R120 / A Place To Dream

parts, T68–69, T94, T104, T132, T431, R6, R9, R60–61
run-on, T81, R62–63
simple and compound, T431, R62–63
word order, R58–59
subjects
and predicates, T68–69, T94, T104, T121, T132, T431, R6, R9, R60–61
simple, compound, complete, T121, T431, R62–63
verbs
gerunds, T262, T293
inflected endings with, T332
tense, T121

Graphic aids
See Graphic organizers.

Graphic organizers
character tree, T66
chart, T19, T30, T41, T48, T71, T73, T102, T144, T151, T156, T177, T181, T183, T191, T208, T233, T261, T262, T294, T298, T306, T314, T333, T341, T388, T389, T405, T416, T418, T423, T424, T438, T451, T458, T470, T478, T499
detectives' log, T73
diagram, T41, T146, T147, T293, T336, T368
knowledge chart, R103
K-W-L chart, T43, T46, T47, T52, T54, T55, T62, T63, T64, T77, T128, T130, T131, T136, T137, R106
map, T41, T56, T59, T112, T113, T184, T205–208, T344, T500
pictograph, T237
prediction chart/diagram, T158, T171, T250, T259, T395, T406, T414, T498, T102
predict-o-gram, T53, T65, T90, T100, R104
prewriting chart, T104, T120, T176
sequence chart/map, T261, T440, T448
story chart/map, T80, T174, T214, T220, T240, T282, T290, T298, T416, T430, R105
story frame, T292, T451
story impressions chart, T316
table, T41
time line, T42
Venn diagram, T419
word grid, T419
word web, T18, T88, T138, T205, T213, T226, T232, T233, T248, T263, T280, T331, T350, T369, T389, T390, T404, T455, T508, R107

Guide words
See Alphabetical order.

Guided reading
See Strategic reading.

Handwriting model, R100–101
Harcourt Brace Library
Unit One: *The Adventures of Ali Baba Bernstein* by Johanna Hurwitz, T9, R39
My Name Is María Isabel by Alma Flor Ada, T9, R39
Unit Two: *Ramona Quimby, Age 8* by Beverly Cleary, T199, R40
Ty's One-Man Band by Mildred Pitts Walter, T199, R40
Unit Three: *Picnic with Piggins* by Jane Yolen, T359, R41
Mush! Across Alaska in the World's Longest Sled-Dog Race by Patricia Seibert, T359, R41

Harcourt Brace Literature Cassettes
See Audiovisual materials.
Health/safety activities, T77, T302, T351
Higher-order thinking skills
See Critical thinking.
Holistic reading assessment
See Assessment options, formal.
Homographs, T139
Homophones, T225
Humor
See Literary elements and techniques.
Humorous fiction
See Literary forms.

Idioms
See Language, diversities of.
Illustrations, using, T13, T19, T20, T24, T58, T83, T135, T158, T163, T166, T203, T369
See also Viewing.
Illustrators, discussing
dePaola, Tomie, T367
Dyer, Jane, T437, T449
Say, Allen, T477, T488
Tiegreen, Alan, T205
Williams, Vera B., T160, T166, T172
Imagery
See Literary elements and techniques.
Independent reading
See Additional reading; Harcourt Brace Library.
Independent reading masters, R108–111
Inferences, making, T11, T22, T29, T47, T56, T58, T63, T97, T101, T116, T137, T145, T169, T170, T201, T217, T253, T254, T256, T260, T276, T285, T286, T291, T320, T322, T330, T373, T379, T382, T383, T387, T416, T445, T450, T466, T489, T504
Informal/performance assessment
See Assessment options, informal.
Informational articles/paragraphs
See Literary forms.
Integrated curriculum
art, T40, T41, T76, T112, T113, T150, T184, T236, T272, T303, T343, T398, T426, T462, T501
health/safety, T77, T302
math, T41, T76, T112, T184, T237, T273, T302, T343, T398, T426, T463
music, T113, T150, T273, T342, T399
physical education, T151, T185
science/technology, T40, T77, T150, T185, T236, T237, T272, T273, T342, T398, T427, T462, T463, T500
social studies, T40, T41, T76, T77, T112, T113, T151, T184, T236, T272, T302, T303, T342, T343, T398, T426, T427, T462, T463, T500, T501
Integrated language arts
grammar, T32, T66, T104, T140, T176, T226, T263, T294, T333, T418, T453, T492
listening, T32, T33, T66, T67, T104, T105, T140, T141, T176, T177, T226, T227, T263, T264, T265, T294, T295, T333, T334, T335, T390, T391, T418, T419, T453, T454, T455, T492, T493
reading, T32, T33, T66, T104, T105, T140, T141, T176, T177, T226, T263, T294, T295, T333, T334, T335, T390, T391, T418, T419, T453, T454, T455, T492
speaking, T33, T66, T104, T105, T140, T141, T176, T177, T226, T227, T263, T264, T265, T294, T295, T333, T334, T335, T390, T391, T418, T419, T453, T454, T455, T493
spelling, T32, T66, T105, T141, T176, T226, T264, T294, T334, T391, T419, T455, T492
viewing, T33, T67, T141, T264, T295, T455, T493
writing, T32, T33, T66, T67, T104, T105, T140, T141, T176, T177, T226, T227, T263, T264, T265, T294, T295, T333, T334, T335, T390, T391, T418, T419, T453, T454, T455, T492, T493
Integrated performance assessment
See Assessment options, formal.
Integrated spelling
See Spelling, integrated.
Interview
See Literary forms; Speaking.

Journal
personal, T20, T29, T47, T54, T63, T83, T90, T118, T158, T188, T203, T208, T243, T250, T275, T282, T316, T363, T370, T387, T406, T433, T440, T465, T468, T480, T506, T508
writing, T30, T37, T64, T71, T102, T118, T138, T145, T174, T198, T207, T224, T233, T261, T269, T292, T299, T331, T339, T352, T358, T388, T395, T416, T425, T451, T459, T468, T490, T506, T512
Judgments, making, T137, T173, T361, T388, T416, T429

Key words
See Vocabulary.
Kinesthetic/motor modality
See Modalities of learning, teaching through; Reteach lessons.
K-W-L strategy, T43, T46, T47, T52, T54, T55, T62, T63, T64, T77, T128, T130, T131, T136, T137, R106

Language
See Grammar; Mechanics.
Language arts activities
See Integrated curriculum; Integrated language arts; Listening; Speaking; Writing.
Language arts connections
See Integrated language arts.
Language Arts Workshop
See Integrated language arts.
Language, diversities of
British English, T408, T417, T427, T440
foreign languages, words from, T24, T280, T281, T282, T284, T303, T446, T491
idioms, T83, T98, T134, T158, T164, T214, T216, T338–339, T417, T484, R26
Spanish literature, T345, T346

INDEX / R121

Language practice
See Daily Language Practice.
Learning disabled students
See Meeting individual needs.
Learning Through the Literature
comprehension, T36–37, T74, T144–145, T183, T232–233, T234, T270, T341, T394–395, T460, T498
comprehension strategy, T38–39, T75, T146–147, T271
decoding strategy, T180–181, T230–231, T300, T340, T397
literary appreciation, T268–269, T298–299, T338–339, T396, T424–425, T458–459
study skills, T70–71, T108–111, T148–149, T182, T301
vocabulary, T422–423, T461, T496–497, T499
vocabulary strategy, T72–73, T235
Legend
See Literary forms.
Letter
See Literary forms.
Library books
See Harcourt Brace Library.
Library materials
See Reference sources; Sources of information.
Limited English proficient students
See Second-language support.
Listening
activities, T32, T33, T66, T67, T76, T104, T105, T112, T113, T115, T124, T126, T140, T141, T150, T151, T152, T184, T185, T186, T188, T189, T227, T254, T272, T342, T345, T399, T400, T427, T462, T463, T511
See also Integrated language arts.
strategies, T10, T173, T200, T306, T348, T360, T430, T470, T508
to literature, T10–11, T200–201, T360–361
Listening/Thinking strategy
See Listening.
Literary appreciation skills
See Literary elements and techniques; Literary forms.
Literary elements and techniques
alliteration, T175
author's craft, T22, T61, T64, T79, T94, T162, T169, T201, T285, T305, T317, T318, T329, T372, T386, T443, T445, T450, T467, T505
author's purpose, T28, T94, T100, T221, T232–233, T270, T372, T449, T467, T470, R20
character
identify major and minor characters, T298–299, T379, T407, T411
interpret character's words, actions, and feelings, T10, T57, T97, T101, T170, T217, T223, T256, T285, T288, T319, T320, T330, T373, T382, T396, T412, T415, T416, T445, T450, T482, T483, T489, T493
characterization
author's description, T104
character's words and actions, T25, T97, T217, T483
conflict, T283, T430
description, T26, T47, T105, T138, T187, T188, T189, T200, T201, T389
dialogue, T226, T239, T240, T430, T453, T482
ending, T240–241
events, T379, T406
fantasy and reality, distinguishing between, T408
humor, T100, T105, T233, T418, T446
idiom
See Language, diversities of.
imagery (sensory images), T188, T189, T200, T201
metaphor, T338–339, R26
mood and tone, T162, T163, T169, T200, T201, T251, T399, T400
narration, T240, T430

onomatopoeia, T295, T452
plot, T208, T240–241, T283, T298–299, T379, T396, T430
point of view
first person, T104, T115, T268–269
third-person, T268–269
problem, T10, T283, T379
rhyme, T151, T176, T465
rhythm, T151
setting, T20, T22, T205, T206, T207, T208, T298–299, T379, T396, T406, T430
simile, T188, T189, T338–339, R26
solution, T240–241
suspense, T440
symbolism, T346
theme, T251
topic sentence, T120, T188
Literary forms
biography, T186
book report/review, T176, T212, T227
descriptive paragraph, T47, T147, T260, T263, T265, T295, T304, T335, T502
fantasy, T117, T513
fiction, T21–28, T55–62, T91–100, T159–172, T187, T215–220, T251–259, T283–290, T317–328, T481–488, T513, R33
humorous fiction, T91–100
informational article/paragraph, T119, T120–121, T140, T226
interview, T120, T221–222, T335, T493
journal/diary, T104
legend, T55–62, T370–386
letter, T32, T78, T177, T185, T191, T236, T302, T348–349, T390
mystery, T433, T438–449, T458–459, T513
myth, T500
narrative, T391, T418
nonfiction, T44–46, T127, T130–136, T140, R33
play, T406–414, T424–425, T442, R31
poetry, T115–118, T196, T275–276, T343, T345–346, T465–468, T493, T503–506
realistic fiction, T21–28, T91–100, T159–172, T193, T215–220, T251–259, T283–290, T317–328, T481–488, T492, T513
riddle, T69, T192, T466
tall tales, T55–62, T66, T67
Literature Cassettes, Harcourt Brace
See Audiovisual materials.
Literature Circles
See Reader response groups.
Literature skills
See Comprehension/Literature skills.
Low-achieving students
See Managing the literature-based classroom; Meeting individual needs.

M

Magazines
See Reference sources.
Main idea and details
introduce, T144–145
review, T234, T341
test, T193
reteach, R13
Mainstreaming, support for
See Meeting individual needs.
Making judgments
See Judgments.

Managing the literature-based classroom, T14, T84, T124, T204, T244, T310, T364, T434, T474
Maps
See Graphic organizers.
Math activities/connections, T41, T76, T92, T112, T184, T237, T273, T302, T343, T398, T426, T463, T501
Mechanics
apostrophe, T241, T318, T349, T390
capitalization
I, T392, R70–71
proper nouns, T178–179, T189, T219, T226, T241, R62–63, R64–65, R68–69
sentences, T23, T32, T34–35, T61, T81, T107, T241, T453, R58–59, R60–61
titles, T509
commas
in addresses, closings, and greetings in letters, T349
in dialogue, T453
contractions, T241
footnotes, T417
friendly letter, format of, T348
indentation of paragraphs, T121, T189
proofreading, R58–75
marks, R57
punctuation
apostrophes, T349
commas, T348, T349, T453
end marks, T23, T32, T34–35, T61, T66, T81, T107, R58–59, R60–61
quotation marks, T453
quotation marks
in dialogue, T453
underlining titles, T509
Meeting individual needs
challenge, T37, T39, T71, T73, T74, T75, T109, T111, T145, T147, T149, T181, T182, T183, T231, T233, T234, T235, T269, T270, T271, T299, T300, T301, T339, T340, T341, T395, T397, T423, T425, T459, T460, T461, T497, T498, T499
gifted and talented students, T14, T84, T124, T204, T244, T310, T364, T434, T474
low-achieving students, T14, T84, T124, T204, T244, T310, T364, T434, T474
mainstreaming, T20, T54, T90, T130, T158, T214, T250, T282, T316, T370, T406, T440, T480
reteach lessons, R1–35
second-language support, T14, T19, T20, T24, T35, T37, T39, T43, T45, T53, T54, T59, T69, T71, T73, T84, T89, T90, T98, T107, T109, T111, T115, T124, T129, T130, T134, T143, T145, T147, T149, T157, T158, T164, T179, T181, T204, T205, T213, T214, T216, T229, T231, T233, T244, T249, T250, T254, T267, T269, T275, T281, T282, T297, T299, T310, T315, T316, T320, T337, T339, T345, T364, T369, T370, T383, T393, T395, T405, T406, T409, T421, T423, T425, T434, T439, T440, T443, T457, T459, T465, T474, T479, T480, T484, T495, T497, T503
special-education students, T14, T84, T124, T204, T244, T310, T364, T434, T474
Meet the Author
See Authors of selections.
Meet the Illustrator
See Illustrators.
Metacognition
See Strategies.
Metaphors
See Literary elements and techniques.
Modalities of learning, teaching through
auditory, T35, T69, T71, T107, T143, T147, T149, T181, T229, T231, T233, T268, T297, T301, T340, T393, T396, T421, T425, T457, T495, T497

R122 / A PLACE TO DREAM

kinesthetic, T35, T37, T69, T71, T73, T107, T109, T145, T149, T182, T231, T234, T267, T271, T297, T299, T300, T301, T337, T393, T397, T421, T457, T495, T497
visual, T35, T37, T39, T69, T71, T73, T74, T107, T109, T143, T145, T147, T149, T179, T181, T182, T183, T229, T231, T233, T235, T267, T269, T270, T271, T297, T300, T301, T337, T339, T393, T395, T397, T421, T423, T425, T457, T459, T495, T497, T499
See also Reteach lessons.
Modeling, T20, T25, T27, T32, T36, T38, T43, T54, T57, T62, T66, T70, T72, T75, T93, T96, T99, T104, T110, T130, T133, T136, T139, T144, T146, T148, T162, T167, T171, T183, T217, T220, T226, T230, T232, T234, T256, T259, T268, T270, T286, T290, T298, T319, T324, T328, T338, T376, T381, T385, T390, T394, T411, T413, T422, T424, T444, T448, T453, T458, T461, T483, T495, T496, T498, T499
See also Think-aloud.
Models of writing forms, R91–99
Mood and tone
See Literary elements and techniques.
Multicultural Connections, T190–191, T350–351, T510–511
See also Cultural awareness; Multicultural Perspectives.
Multicultural Perspectives, T42, T78, T114, T152, T186, T238, T274, T304, T344, T400, T428, T464, T502
See also Cultural awareness; Multicultural Connections.
Multiple-meaning words, T26, T253, T275, T443
Music activities, T67, T113, T123, T126, T128, T130, T131, T137, T138, T140, T141, T143, T150, T151, T152, T160, T168, T177, T184, T185, T186, T188, T189, T227, T273, T342, T399, T501
Mystery
See Literary forms.
Myth
See Literary forms.

Narration
See Literary elements and techniques.
Narrative
See Literary forms.
Newspapers
See Reference sources.
Nonfiction
See Literary forms.
Nouns
common
introduce, T142–143
review, T164, T176
test, T193
reteach, R12
plural (-*ies* ending) and irregular
introduce, T266–267
review, T287, T294
test, T353
reteach, R21
possessive, plural
introduce, T336–337
review, T384, T390
test, T353
reteach, R25
possessive, singular
introduce, T296–297

review, T318, T333
test, T353
reteach, R23
proper
introduce, T178–179
review, T219, T226
test, T193
reteach, R16
See also Mechanics.
singular and plural (-*s* and -*es* endings)
introduce, T228–229
review, T258, T263
test, T353
reteach, R18
See also Grammar.

Onomatopoeia
See Literary elements and techniques.
Options for reading, T20, T54, T90, T130, T158, T214, T250, T282, T316, T370, T406, T440, T480
Oral language activities
See Speaking; Speaking and oral reading, guidelines for.
Oral rereading, T66, T104, T140, T176, T226, T263, T294, T333, T390, T453, T492
See also Readers Theatre.
Organizing information, T19, T30, T41, T48, T66, T71, T73, T80, T88, T101, T102, T104, T120, T138, T144, T147, T151, T156, T174, T176, T177, T183, T188, T191, T208, T212, T226, T233, T248, T250, T259, T261, T263, T282, T290, T294, T298, T306, T314, T316, T332, T333, T335, T336, T341, T343, T344, T348, T404, T405, T406, T414, T416, T418, T419, T424

Pacing, T6, T14, T84, T124, T196, T204, T244, T310, T356, T364, T434, T474
Partner reading
See Reader response groups.
Parts of speech
See Grammar.
Performance assessment
See Assessment options.
Period
See Mechanics.
Personal Journal
See Journal, personal.
Personal response, T29, T47, T63, T101, T137, T173, T207, T223, T260, T291, T330, T387, T415, T450, T468, T489
Photographs, discussing, T77, T186, T191
Physical education activities, T151, T185
Plays, elements of
introduce, T424–425
reteach, R31
See also Literary forms.
Plot
See Literary elements and techniques; Story elements.
Poems in Anthology
"Closed, I am a mystery," T466
"Hello, Book!" T466

"Lisa's Fingerprints," T116
"People," T504
"Some People," T505
"Versos sencillos" ("Simple Verses"), T346
"Who Am I?" T117
"Would you like," T467
"Writers," T276
Poetry
reading, T115–118, T275–276, T345–346, T465–468, T493, T503–506
reciting, T236
writing, T196, T275, T343, T345, T465, T493
See also Literary forms.
Poets in Anthology
Bodecker, N. M., T465
Field, Rachel, T503, T505
Holman, Felice, T115
Little, Jean, T275
Livingston, Myra Cohn, T465
Martí, José, T345
Morrison, Lillian, T465
O'Neill, Mary, T115
Zolotow, Charlotte, T503
Point of view
introduce, T268–269
reteach, R22
See also Literary elements and techniques.
Portfolio
See Assessment options, reading/writing portfolio.
Portfolio conference
See Assessment options, informal.
Predicates
See Grammar; Sentences, parts of (predicate).
Predicates and subjects
See Grammar; Subjects and predicates.
Predictions, making
introduce, T394–395
review, T460, T498
test, T513
reteach, R28
See also Predictions, making and confirming; Preview and predict.
Predictions, making and confirming, T9, T13, T20, T21, T25, T27, T54, T55, T57, T62, T83, T90, T91, T93, T96, T99, T100, T115, T130, T131, T133, T136, T158, T159, T162, T167, T171, T194, T205, T206, T214, T215, T217, T220, T251, T256, T259, T283, T285, T286, T288, T290, T317, T319, T324, T328, T370, T371, T376, T381, T385, T395, T406, T407, T411, T413, T414, T433, T441, T444, T447, T448, T465, T480, T481, T483, T487
See also Preview and predict.
Prefixes
See Structural analysis; Structural and contextual clues; Structural clues.
Prereading strategies, T20, T54, T90, T130, T158, T214, T250, T282, T316, T370, T406, T440
Preview and predict, T20, T90, T130, T158, T203, T214, T232, T243, T250, T282, T309, T316, T370, T406, T440, T480
See also Predictions, making; Predictions, making and confirming.
Prewriting
See Process writing steps; Writer's Workshop.
Prior knowledge
See Background.
Problem
See Literary elements and techniques.
Process writing steps
prewriting, T80, T120, T188, T240, T306, T348, T430, T470, T508
drafting, T80, T120, T188, T240, T306, T348, T430, T470, T508
responding and revising, T79, T80, T120, T188, T204, T240, T306, T348, T430, T470, T508

INDEX / R123

proofreading, T79, T81, T121, T189, T241, T307, T349, T431, T471, T509
publishing, T81, T119, T121, T189, T204, T241, T307, T349, T431, T471, T509
Project Cards, T26, T33, T41, T56, T60, T67, T77, T92, T97, T104, T105, T112, T113, T135, T140, T141, T150, T151, T160, T168, T176, T177, T184, T185, T186, T218, T219, T226, T227, T236, T237, T238, T257, T263, T265, T272, T274, T284, T294, T295, T302, T303, T325, T333, T335, T342, T343, T375, T377, T390, T391, T410, T419, T426, T427, T428, T443, T446, T453, T454, T462, T463, T484, T486, T493, T500, T502
Pronouns
  object
    introduce, T456–457
    review, T485, T492
    test, T513
    reteach, R32
  singular and plural
    introduce, T392–393
    review, T412, T418
    test, T513
    reteach, R27
  subject
    introduce, T420–421
    review, T447, T453
    test, T513
    reteach, R29
  See also Grammar.
Proofreading
  See Mechanics; Process writing steps; Writer's Workshop.
Proper nouns
  See Grammar; Nouns, proper.
Publishing
  See Process writing steps; Writer's Workshop.
Punctuation
  See Mechanics.
Purpose, author's
  See Author's purpose.
Purpose for listening, T10, T200, T360
Purpose for reading
  returning to, T27, T46, T62, T100, T115, T136, T171, T190, T206, T220, T259, T275, T290, T328, T345, T385, T414, T448, T465, T487, T503
  setting a, T8, T20, T21, T25, T43, T54, T55, T57, T90, T91, T115, T133, T158, T159, T198, T205, T214, T215, T250, T256, T275, T282, T283, T286, T316, T317, T319, T324, T345, T370, T371, T406, T407, T411, T440, T441, T444, T465, T480, T481, T503

Quickwrite, T18, T52, T88, T128, T156, T248, T280, T368, T438, T478
Quotations, direct quotation/dialogue
  See Mechanics.

Read aloud,
  student, T35, T66, T104, T105, T115, T119, T121, T189, T191, T233, T241, T263, T294, T333, T345, T391, T418, T431, T492, T503, T509

teacher, T14, T20, T42, T67, T78, T90, T114, T115, T130, T152, T186, T200–201, T214, T238, T272, T274, T275, T282, T304, T344, T345, T360–361, T400, T406, T419, T428, T440, T462, T464, T465, T480, T502
  See also Listening to literature; Oral rereading.
Reader Response Cards, T21, T55, T91, T131, T159, T215, T251, T283, T317, T371, T407, T441, T481, R77–88
Reader response groups
  collaborative response, T317, T330, T371, T387
  literature circles, T21, T29, T55, T63, T131, T159, T173, T215, T223, T251, T260, T283, T291, T407, T415, T441, T450
  partner reading, T91, T101, T481, T489
Readers Theatre, T140, T226
Reader-Writer Connection, T233, T269, T339, T425, T459
Reading corner, T124
Reading rate, adjusting, T20
  See also Active reading strategies; Strategic reading, suggestions for.
Reading skills assessment
  See Assessment options, formal.
Reading strategies
  See Strategies.
Reading/writing portfolio
  See Assessment options, informal.
Realistic fiction
  See Literary forms.
Reference sources
  almanac, T41, T112
  atlas, T41, T110
  autobiographies, T351
  biographies, T351
  brochures, T194
  calendar, T112
  card catalog, T110, T111
  catalogs, T273, T511
  dictionary, T33, T72, T105, T108, T109, T110, T134, T139, T181, T189, T192, T480
  encyclopedia, T47, T108, T110, T140, T185, T191, T272, T343, T351, T419, T427, T462, T500
  globe, T190
  glossary, T33, T72, T109, T515
  library materials, T47, T77, T103, T110, T120, T140, T177, T185, T191, T237, T398
  newspapers and magazines, T120, T191, T192, T273, T351, T421, T495, T511
  specialized reference sources, T272
  telephone directory, T108, T110, T191, T302
  thesaurus, T189, T192, T389
  videos, T120
  See also Sources of information.
Research, T40, T41, T42, T77, T78, T114, T120, T140, T141, T151, T177, T184, T185, T186, T191, T194, T236, T237, T238, T272, T274, T342, T343, T344, T351, T391, T398, T400, T419, T426, T427, T428, T462, T463, T500, T501, T502, T511
Resources, additional
  graphic organizers, R102–107
  handwriting models, R100–101
  independent reading masters, R108–111
  models of writing forms, R91–99
Responding and revising
  See Process writing steps; Writer's Workshop.
Response cards
  See Reader Response Cards.
Reteach lessons
  active reading strategies, R5
  adjectives, R34
  alphabetical order, R10
  author's purpose, R20
  cause and effect, R4

  context clues, R30
  directions, following, R7
  fiction and nonfiction, R33
  figurative language, R26
  main idea and details, R13
  nouns, common, R12
  nouns, plural (-ies ending) and irregular, R21
  nouns, possessive plural, R25
  nouns, possessive singular, R23
  nouns, proper, R16
  nouns, singular and plural (-s and -es endings), R18
  plays, elements of, R31
  point of view, R22
  predictions, making, R28
  pronouns (object), R32
  pronouns (singular and plural), R27
  pronouns (subject), R29
  sentence parts (predicate), R9
  sentence parts (subject), R6
  sentences, kinds of, R3
  sources of information, R11
  story elements, R24
  structural analysis, R19
  structural and contextual clues, R8
  structural clues, R17
  synonyms, antonyms, and analogies, R35
  synthesizing ideas, R14
  test-taking strategies, R15
Retelling, T30, T100, T102, T138
Retelling, oral/written
  See Assessment options, informal.
Rhyme
  See Literary elements and techniques.
Rhythm
  See Literary elements and techniques.
Riddles
  See Literary forms.
Running records
  See Assessment options, informal.
Run-ons
  See Grammar.

Scanning
  See Test-taking strategies.
Science/technology activities, T40, T45, T46, T48, T77, T150, T185, T191, T236, T237, T257, T272, T273, T342, T375, T398, T427, T443, T462, T463, T500, T511
Scope and sequence, R113–118
Second-language support
  diagrams or pictures, creating, T37, T204, T244, T267
  discussion, T20, T39, T43, T59, T71, T84, T129, T205, T250, T254, T269, T282, T316, T459, T465, T495
  figurative language, T339
  grammar, T69, T107, T179, T229, T297, T337, T393, T421, T434, T457, T474
  idioms, T98, T134, T158, T164, T214, T216, T339, T484
  illustrations and photographs, using, T19, T130, T339, T369, T503
  listening to selections, T124
  mechanics, T35
  multiple-meaning words, T275, T443
  pantomime, T45, T157, T249, T288, T320
  punctuation, using English-language, T310
  realia, using, T134, T143
  role-playing, T425

skills, T109, T111, T145, T147, T149, T233
strategic reading, T20, T54, T90, T370
vocabulary, T14, T24, T53, T73, T89, T115, T164, T181, T213, T231, T281, T299, T315, T383, T405, T406, T409, T423, T439, T440, T479, T480, T497

Selections in Anthology
legend
"Legend of the Indian Paintbrush, The," T365–400
map
"Ramona's Neighborhood," T205–208
mystery
"Piggins," T435–464
nonfiction
"Meet the Orchestra," T125–152
"Seed Is a Promise, A," T43–48
play
"Paddington Paints a Picture," T401–428
realistic fiction
"Adventures of Ali Baba Bernstein, The," T85–114
"Gift for Tía Rosa, A," T277–304
"Justin and the Best Biscuits in the World," T311–344
"Lost Lake, The," T475–502
"Miss Rumphius," T15–42
"Music, Music for Everyone," T153–186
"Ramona Quimby, Age 8," T209–238
"Through Grandpa's Eyes," T245–274
riddles
"Closed, I am a mystery," T465–466, T468
tall tale
"Johnny Appleseed," T49–78
See also Poems in Anthology.

Selections in Teacher's Guide
"Benjamin Banneker's Wooden Clock," T10–11
"Case of the Earthenware Pig, The," T360–361
"Good Morning, River!" T200–201

Self-esteem, building students', T354

Sentences
kinds of (declarative, exclamatory, imperative, interrogative)
introduce, T34–35
review, T23, T32, T61, T66
test, T193
reteach, R3
See also Mechanics.
parts of (predicate)
introduce, T106–107
review, T132, T140
test, T193
reteach, R9
parts of (subject)
introduce, T68–69
review, T94, T104
test, T193
reteach, R6
See also Grammar.
simple and compound
See Grammar.

Sequence, T306, T430

Setting
See Literary elements and techniques; Story elements.

Setting a purpose
See Purpose for listening; Purpose for reading.

Simile
See Figurative language; Literary elements and techniques.

Skills assessment
See Assessment options, formal.

Social studies activities, T23, T40, T41, T56, T60, T76, T77, T78, T112, T113, T135, T141, T151, T184, T190, T191, T206, T236, T255, T272, T289, T302, T303, T325, T342, T343, T351, T378, T398, T409, T426, T427, T446, T462, T463, T500, T501, T502, T511

Solution
See Literary elements and techniques.

Sources of information (card catalog)
introduce, T110–111
reteach, R11
See also Reference sources.

Spanish words/literature
See Language, diversities of.

Speaking
book report, T105
description, T201
discussion, T8, T13, T48, T78, T79, T83, T113, T114, T115, T118, T119, T137, T152, T186, T203, T208, T236, T238, T239, T261, T274, T304, T305, T344, T347, T388, T391, T400, T428, T464, T469, T473, T502
drama, T11, T418
interview, T335, T454, T493
oral report/presentation, T33, T77, T141, T177, T184, T185, T186, T191, T236, T237, T295, T335, T342, T391, T427, T462, T463
paraphrasing, T172
Readers Theatre, T140, T226
recitation, T236
recording on audiotape, T471
role-playing, T14, T30, T224, T227, T265, T292, T419, T454, T490
speech, T227, T493
storytelling, T334, T431
telephone conversation, T361

Speaking and oral reading, guidelines for, T32, T104, T121, T140, T227, T236, T263, T390, T503

Special education students
See Meeting individual needs.

Spelling, integrated
review, T32, T66, T105, T141, T192, T226, T264, T294, T334, T352, T419, T455, T492, T512, R58–75
spelling-vocabulary connection, T19, T53, T89, T129, T157, T213, T249, T281, T315, T369, T405, T439, T479

Story elements (plot, setting, characters)
introduce, T298–299
review, T396
reteach, R24
See also Literary elements and techniques.

Story map
See Graphic organizers.

Strategic reading, suggestions for, T21, T25, T27, T43, T55, T57, T62, T91, T93, T96, T99, T131, T133, T136, T159, T162, T167, T171, T205, T215, T217, T220, T251, T256, T259, T283, T286, T290, T317, T319, T324, T328, T371, T376, T381, T407, T411, T413, T441, T444, T448, T481, T483, T486
See also Active reading strategies; K-W-L strategy; Preview and predict; Purpose for reading.

Strategies
See Active reading strategies; Context clues; K-W-L strategy; Preview and predict; Purpose for reading; Structural analysis; Structural and contextual clues; Structural clues; Synonyms, antonyms, analogies; Synthesizing ideas.

Strategy conference
See Assessment options, informal.

Structural analysis
introduce, T230–231
review, T300, T340
maintain, T397
test, T353
reteach, R19

Structural and contextual clues
introduce, T72–73
review, T235

reteach, R8
See also Context clues; Structural analysis; Structural clues.

Structural clues
introduce, T180–181
reteach, R17
See also Context clues; Structural analysis; Structural and contextual clues.

Student self-assessment
See Assessment options, informal.

Students acquiring English
See Second-language support.

Students at risk
See Meeting individual needs, low-achieving students.

Study skills
See Alphabetical order; Directions; Sources of information; Test-taking strategies.

Subjects and predicates
See Grammar; Sentences, kinds of (predicate); Sentences, kinds of (subject).

Subjects (simple, compound, complete)
See Grammar.

Suffixes
See Structural analysis; Structural and contextual clues; Structural clues.

Summarizing, T11, T25, T27, T58, T67, T75, T173, T189, T241, T286, T393, T451, T457, T459, T463, T486
See also Assessment options, informal; Summarizing the literature.

Summarizing the literature
character chart, T30
journal frame, T331
K-W-L chart, T47, T64
sequence chain/chart, T224, T261
story frame, T102, T292, T451
story map, T174, T388, T416, T490
web, T138
written summary, T224, T261, T292, T331, T416
See also Assessment options, informal.

Suspense
See Literary elements and techniques.

Sustained silent reading, T250, T282, T316, T370, T406, T440, T480

Symbolism
See Literary elements and techniques.

Synonyms, antonyms, analogies, T59, T89, T175, T192, T249, T281, T315, T405, T439, T443, T452, T479
introduce, T496–497
reteach, R35

Synthesizing ideas, T63, T101, T260, T290, T324, T387
introduce, T146–147
reteach, R14

T

Tall tales
See Literary forms.

Teacher read-aloud
See Read aloud.

Teacher resources, T194, T354, T514
See also Resources.

Teaching tips, T44, T115, T160, T205, T216, T275, T372, T404, T408, T442, T446, T482
See also Managing the literature-based classroom; Teacher resources.

INDEX / R125

Telephone directory
  See Reference sources.
Testing and management
  See Assessment options, formal; Assessment options, informal; Assessment options, student self-assessment; Managing the literature-based classroom.
Test-taking strategies
  introduce, T148–149
  reteach, R15
Themes in Anthology
  introducing, T6, T12–13, T82–83, T122–123, T196, T202–203, T242–243, T308–309, T356, T362–363, T432–433, T472–473
  themes
    Being Different, T82–121
    Caring and Sharing, T242–307
    Great Outdoors, The, T472–509
    Learning About Yourself, T308–349
    Listen to This! T122–189
    Mysteries to Solve, T432–471
    Picture This!, T362–431
    Planting a Seed, T12–81
    School Days, T202–241
  wrap-up, T79, T119, T187, T239, T305, T347, T429, T469, T507
  See also Literary elements and techniques.
Thesaurus
  See Reference sources.
Think-aloud, T20, T25, T27, T36, T43, T57, T62, T72, T75, T93, T96, T99, T110, T144, T146, T148, T162, T167, T171, T217, T220, T230, T232, T256, T259, T268, T286, T290, T298, T319, T324, T328, T338, T376, T381, T385, T394, T411, T413, T422, T424, T444, T448, T458, T461, T483, T486, T496
Thinking strategies
  See Creative thinking; Critical thinking; Modeling; Think-aloud.
Topic
  See Literary elements and techniques; Main idea and details.
Trade books
  See Additional reading; Harcourt Brace Library.

Units
  introducing, T6–9, T196–199, T356–359
  units
    Unit 1: Being Special, T5–194
    Unit 2: Friendships, T195–354
    Unit 3: Adventures, T355–514
  wrap-up, T192–193, T352–353, T512–513

Verbs, tenses
  See Grammar.
Videos
  See Reference sources.
Viewing, T13, T33, T40, T41, T76, T83, T115, T141, T184, T186, T191, T203, T237, T272, T297, T343, T398, T418, T419, T426, T427, T428, T462, T463, T495, T501
Visual modality
  See Modalities of learning, teaching through; Reteach lessons.
Visualizing, T40, T41, T44, T133, T254, T271, T272, T331, T343, T441, T442, T450, T511
Vocabulary
  extending, T31, T65, T103, T139, T175, T225, T262, T293, T332, T389, T417, T452, T491
  introducing, T18, T19, T52, T53, T88, T89, T128, T129, T156, T157, T212, T213, T248, T249, T280, T281, T314, T315, T368, T369, T404, T405, T438, T439, T478, T479
  reviewing, T31, T65, T103, T139, T175, T192, T225, T262, T293, T332, T352, T389, T417, T452, T491, T512
  strategies, T18–19, T26, T44, T52–53, T59, T88–89, T95, T128–129, T132, T156–157, T165, T212–213, T235, T248–249, T253, T280–281, T287, T314–315, T321, T323, T368–369, T374, T404–405, T422–423, T438–439, T478–479, T484
  testing, T7, T197, T513
Vocabulary strategies
  See Context clues; Structural and contextual clues; Synonyms, antonyms, analogies.
  See also Decoding strategies; Multiple-meaning words.
Vocabulary Workshop
  See Vocabulary, extending.

W

Word lists
  See Vocabulary, introducing.
Word parts
  See Structural analysis; Structural and contextual clues.
Writer's Workshop
  book review, T508–509
  descriptive paragraph, T188–189
  friendly letter, T348–349
  how-to paragraph, T306–307
  new ending for story, T240–241
  paragraph of information, T120–121
  personal narrative, T80–81
  persuasive paragraph, T470–471
  story, T430–431
Writing
  advertisement, T223, T233, T455, T512
  biography, T186
  book of ideas, T33
  book review, T176
  Braille messages, T264
  brochure, T426
  captions, T41
  clues, T459
  comic strip, T35, T512
  commercial, T227
  critique, T428
  customs, about, T303
  description, T47, T113, T140, T145, T147, T260, T263, T265, T275, T295, T304, T335, T502
  dialogue, T453
  directions, T71, T113, T295, T512
  foreign language dictionary, T303
  garden journal, T77
  glossary of terms related to ships, T33
  handbook, T236
  letter, T32, T78, T177, T185, T191, T236, T302, T390
  list, T78, T101, T212, T265, T438
  lyrics, T399
  mystery story, T459
  news story, T63
  opinions of music, T137
  pamphlet, T419
  paragraph, T48, T67, T105, T107, T186, T234, T275, T291, T339, T351, T387
  paragraph of comparison and contrast, T330, T419
  paragraph of information, T140, T226, T270
  paragraph of opinion, T450
  personal narrative, T391, T418
  poem, T196, T275, T343, T345, T465, T493
  point of view, writing from a different, T269, T275
  postcard, T489
  recipes, T335
  report, T40, T41, T76, T141, T398, T427, T500
  review of a performance, T143
  scene, T334
  scene directions, T425
  secret code, messages in, T434
  story, T35, T37, T78, T105, T233, T264, T294, T299, T352, T370, T492
  story ending, T333, T415
  story problems, T237
  survival guide, T342
  tips on staying healthy, T302
  See also Quickwrite; Summarizing the literature; Writer's Workshop.
Writing and language skills assessment
  See Assessment options, formal.
Writing models, R91–99
Writing process
  See Process writing steps; Writer's Workshop.

R126 / A PLACE TO DREAM

Reviewers and Advisors
FIELD TEST SITES, MULTICULTURAL ADVISORS, CRITICAL REVIEWERS

Field Test Sites

Fyffe, Alabama
Vinemont, Alabama
Phoenix, Arizona
Cabot, Arkansas
Conway, Arkansas
Moreno Valley, California
Riverside, California
Sacramento, California
San Diego, California
San Francisco, California
Bridgeport, Connecticut
Lisbon, Connecticut
New Haven, Connecticut
Gainesville, Florida
Homestead, Florida
Jacksonville, Florida
Land O'Lakes, Florida
Orlando, Florida
Tampa, Florida
Pocatello, Idaho
Mahomet, Illinois
Naperville, Illinois
Gosport, Indiana
Spencer, Indiana
Donnellson, Iowa
Kansas City, Kansas
Mount Sterling, Kentucky
Bossier City, Louisiana
Rising Sun, Maryland
Bridgman, Michigan
Detroit, Michigan
Robbinsdale, Minnesota
St. Louis, Missouri
Billings, Montana
Nashua, New Hampshire
North Bergen, New Jersey
Chaparral, New Mexico
Las Cruces, New Mexico
Bronx, New York
Brooklyn, New York
Cincinnati, Ohio
New Carlisle, Ohio
Toledo, Ohio
University Heights, Ohio
Oklahoma City, Oklahoma
Beaverton, Oregon
Eugene, Oregon
Portland, Oregon
Fairless Hills, Pennsylvania
N. Huntingdon, Pennsylvania
Philadelphia, Pennsylvania
Estill, South Carolina
Greer, South Carolina
Aberdeen, South Dakota
Pine Ridge, South Dakota
Porcupine, South Dakota
Brentwood, Tennessee
Nashville, Tennessee
Corsicana, Texas
Dallas, Texas
Grand Prairie, Texas
Harlingen, Texas
Houston, Texas
Katy, Texas
Lewisville, Texas
Lockhart, Texas
McAllen, Texas
Palestine, Texas
Plano, Texas
San Antonio, Texas
Dry Fork, Virginia
Midlothian, Virginia
Everett, Washington
Vancouver, Washington
Athens, West Virginia
Green Bay, Wisconsin
Waukesha, Wisconsin

Multicultural Advisors

Dr. James E. Anderson
Associate Professor, Department of Educational Leadership and Cultural Studies
College of Education
University of Houston
Houston, Texas

Dr. Mario Benitez
Professor, Department of Curriculum and Instruction
The University of Texas at Austin
Austin, Texas

Dr. Pat Browne
Director, African-American History/Multicultural Education
Indianapolis, Public Schools
Indianapolis, Indiana

Dr. Jacob Carruthers
Associate Director and Professor
Northeastern Illinois University Center for Inner City Studies
Chicago, Illinois

Dr. Nancy Mayeda
Principal
Rooftop Alternative School
San Francisco, California

Dr. Maria E. Morales
Associate Professor and Director of Undergraduate Bilingual Education Program
Undergraduate Teacher Preparation Program
Texas A & I University
Kingsville, Texas

Dr. Cornel Pewewardy
Principal
Mounds Park All-Nations Magnet School
St. Paul, Minnesota

Dr. Rudy Rodriguez
Professor and Chair, Department of Reading and Bilingual Education
College of Education and Human Ecology
Texas Woman's University
Denton, Texas

Sherry Sellers
Librarian and Multicultural Specialist
Detroit, Michigan

Dr. Barbara Shin
Principal
Andersen Contemporary School
Minneapolis, Minnesota

Virginia Driving Hawk Sneve
Secondary Counselor
Indian Education and District Resource for Native-American Culture
Rapid City, South Dakota

Charlotte Stokes
Teacher Specialist—Social Studies
Alexandria City Public Schools
Alexandria, Virginia

Dr. Bernida Thompson
Principal
Roots Activity Learning Center
Washington, District of Columbia

Marilys Tognetti
Director of Instruction
Dixon Unified School District
Dixon, California

Critical Reviewers

Ginger Abel
Teacher
Peoria Public Schools
Peoria, Illinois

Natalie Ahern
Teacher
John F. Kennedy School
Westfield, NJ

C. Gloria Akers
Educational Consultant
James Rhoads School
Philadelphia, Pennsylvania

Claudia Anderson
Teacher
Solheim Elementary
Bismarck, North Dakota

Margo Angleton
Teacher
Indialantic Elementary
Melbourne, Florida

Karyn Aulwurm
Coordinator, Teacher Training and Staff Development
Clark County School District
Las Vegas, Nevada

Hilda Barrett
Teacher
Harper's Choice Middle School
Columbia, Maryland

Kristi Baur
Resource Teacher
West Windsor/Plainsboro Upper Elementary
Cronburg, NJ

Diana Bauske
Teacher
Richland Elementary
Richardson, Texas

Florence T. Carter
Teacher
Campbell School
Metuchen, New Jersey

Becky Cebula
Reading Specialist
Cecil Co. Public Schools
Elkton, MD

Cicely Cerqui
Coordinator for Elementary Curriculum
Shoreline Public Schools
Seattle, Washington

Cheryl Clemens
Language Arts Supervisor
Savannah Chatham Board of Education Riley Annex
Savannah, GA

Pam Coleman
Teacher
Lee's Summit, MO

Lenore Croudy
Coordinator of Language Arts and Humanities
Flint Community Schools
Flint, Michigan

Fern Davis
Teacher
Mandarin Oaks Elementary School
Jacksonville, FL

Dr. Carol DeRita
Teacher
Porter Elementary
Mesquite, Texas

Judith DeStefano-Anen
Assistant Principal/Reading Specialist
Ella G. Clarke School
Lakewood, New Jersey

Marilyn Dickey
Language Arts Specialist
Shelton View Elementary
Bothell, Washington

Sheila Durante, RSM
Assistant Superintendent for Elementary Schools
Diocese of Providence
Providence, Rhode Island

Mary Ellen Everitt
Teacher
Antheil Elementary
Trenton, New Jersey

Lisa Fast
Teacher
Escola Americana do Rio de Janeiro, Brazil

Shirley Fields
District Reading Coordinator
Miami, Florida

Bettie Fitzhenry
Reading Consultant
Killeen Independent School District
Killeen, Texas

Ann Carol Franco
Teacher
American School Foundation
Mexico City, Mexico

Janet Green
Teacher
Whitehouse Primary School
Whitehouse, Ohio

Rilla Hardgrove
Principal
Meadow Lark School
Billings, Montana

Sister Patricia Healey, IHM
Elementary Supervisor
Sisters of the Immaculate Heart of Mary
Philadelphia, Pennsylvania

Sandra Hetzel
Teacher
Solheim Elementary
Bismarck, North Dakota

Don Hillyard
Reading Coordinator
Evansville-Vanderburgh Schools
Evansville, Indiana

Daisy Howard-Douglas
Teacher
Fairfield Court Elementary
Richmond, Virginia

Corine Howell
Chapter I
St. Vincent Catholic School
Most Pure Heart of Mary
Mobile, AL

William James
Principal
Orange Center Elementary
Orlando, Florida

Karen Jao
Teacher
Taipei American School
Taipei, Taiwan

Dr. Mary Whisonant Jennings
Teacher
Tubman Elementary
Washington, District of Columbia

Beth Kealy
Teacher
Patterson Elementary
Eugene, Oregon

Jan Keese
District Reading Chair
Ankeny Community Schools
Ankeny, Iowa

Laressa Jane Kschinka
Teacher
American School of The Hague
Wassenaar, The Netherlands

Maya Lagbara, Ed.D.
Assistant Principal
Spruce High School
Dallas, Texas

Elizabeth Lolli
Coordinator, Elementary Education
Middletown City Schools
Middletown, Ohio

Joyce London
Reading Specialist
Southard School
Howell, New Jersey

Bertha Long-Jackson
Teacher
Jesse Owens School
South Holland, Illinois

Ida Love, Ph.D.
Assistant Superintendent of Education Support Services
Kansas City, Missouri School District
Kansas City, Missouri

Constance Major
Reading Specialist
Shawmont School
Philadelphia, Pennsylvania

Tracy Matthews
Teacher
Linden Elementary School
Oakridge, TN

Jana McCarthy
Language Arts Coordinator
Meridian School District
Meridian, Idaho

Mary K. McCarthy
Reading Specialist
Owyhee Elementary
The Independent School District of Boise City
Boise, Idaho

Bonnie McIntyre
Curriculum Coordinator
Minneapolis Public Schools
Minneapolis, Minnesota

Carlton Mead
Student Supervisor
Aloha Park Elementary
Beaverton, Oregon

Dr. Jacqueline Mossburg
Coordinator, Staff Development
Fort Wayne Community Schools
Fort Wayne, Indiana

Charlotte J. Parks
Teacher
Windsor Elementary
Des Moines Independent Community School District
Des Moines, Iowa

Beth Peterson
Teacher
Mount Tabor Elementary
New Albany, Indiana

Evelyn Pittman
Supervisor of Language Arts
Paterson Public Schools
Paterson, New Jersey

Kaye Price-Hawkins
Consultant
Region XIV
Abilene, Texas

Tamara Jo Rhomberg
Reading Specialist
Garlin Kellison Elementary
Fenton, Missouri

David Rubin
Supervisor of Reading
Gateway Center
New Haven, Connecticut

Blanche Ryan
Supervisor of Reading
Indianapolis Public Schools
Indianapolis, Indiana

Janet Sawyer
Teacher
Highland Park Elementary
Austin, Texas

James F. Schindler, Ed.D.
Curriculum Consultant
Jordan School District
Sandy, Utah

Jan Scott
Curriculum Coordinator, K-3
Bossier Parish School System
Bossier City, Louisiana

Sheila Scott
Program Assistant
Cora Howe Elementary
Nashville, Tennessee

Marsha Shortt
Teacher
Stewart Elementary
Kemah, Texas

Sheldon Shuch, Ph.D.
Director of Instruction and Professional Development
Community School District Five
New York, New York

Wanda Smithie
Teacher
Oak Park Elementary School
Biloxi, MS

Wilma Taylor
Teacher
Catherine C. Blackwell Institute
Detroit, MI

Susan Totaro
Teacher
West Windsor/Plainsboro Upper Elementary
Plainsboro, NJ

Patti Van der Have
Principal
Bonita Springs, FL

Richard Wagner
Language Arts Curriculum Coordinator
Paradise Valley School District
Phoenix, Arizona

Sister Mary Leanne Welch, PBVM
Curriculum Director
Archdiocese of Dubuque
Dubuque, Iowa

Jackie Williams
Instructional Supervisor
Loudon County Schools
Loudon, Tennessee

Lola Williams, Ed.D.
Bilingual Coordinator
Harlingen Consolidated Independent School District
Harlingen, Texas

Louverne I. Williams
Teacher
Holland School
Minneapolis, Minnesota

Sara Jane Wilson
Teacher
Landis Elementary
Alief, Texas

Sister Marla Ann Yeck, RSM, Ph.D.
Director of Education
Sisters of Mercy of the Americas
Silver Spring, Maryland

Parent Reviewers

Gail Adler
Ft. Worth, Texas

Linda Curry
Bloomfield Hills, Michigan

Ian Fingerman
Skokie, Illinois

Louis Guerrero
Dallas, Texas

Rachel Guerrero
Dallas, Texas

Patricia Hales
Salt Lake City, Utah

Randa Henry
Coeur d'Alene, Idaho

Jo A. Jorgenson
Phoenix, Arizona

Kay Morton
Dallas, Texas

Sandy Nickley
Dayton, Ohio

Sharon Wille
Highlands Ranch, Colorado

Acknowledgments

For permission to reprint copyrighted material, grateful acknowledgment is made to the following sources:

Bradbury Press, an Affiliate of Macmillan, Inc.: Cover illustration by Rick Brown from *Kate Heads West* by Pat Brisson. Illustration copyright © 1990 by Rick Brown. Cover illustration from *Mozart Tonight* by Julie Downing. Copyright © 1991 by Julie Downing. Cover illustration by Pat Cummings from *Mariah Loves Rock* by Mildred Pitts Walter. Illustration copyright © 1990 by Pat Cummings.

Carolrhoda Books, Inc., Minneapolis, MN: Cover illustration by Hannu Taina from *Mister King* by Raija Siekkinen, translated by Tim Steffa. Illustration copyright © 1986 by Hannu Taina.

Clarion Books, a Houghton Mifflin Company imprint: Cover illustration from *June 29, 1999* by David Wiesner. Copyright © 1992 by David Wiesner.

Coward-McCann, Inc.: Cover illustration by Bruce Degen from *Commander Toad and the Intergalactic Spy* by Jane Yolen. Illustration copyright © 1986 by Bruce Degen.

Dial Books for Young Readers, a division of Penguin Books USA Inc.: Cover illustration by Brad Sneed from *Grandpa's Song* by Tony Johnston. Illustration copyright © 1991 by Bradley D. Sneed. Cover illustration from *Prehistoric Pinkerton* by Steven Kellogg. Copyright © 1987 by Steven Kellogg. Cover illustration from *The Island of the Skog* by Steven Kellogg. Copyright © 1973 by Steven Kellogg. Cover illustration from *Pinkerton, Behave!* by Steven Kellogg. Copyright © 1979 by Steven Kellogg.

Farrar, Straus & Giroux, Inc.: Cover illustration from *Brave Irene* by William Steig. Copyright © 1986 by William Steig.

Greenwillow Books, a division of William Morrow & Company, Inc.: Cover illustration by Yossi Abolafia from *Harry in Trouble* by Barbara Ann Porte. Illustration copyright © 1989 by Yossi Abolafia. Cover illustration from *A Chair for My Mother* by Vera B. Williams. Copyright © 1982 by Vera B. Williams. Cover illustration from *Something Special for Me* by Vera B. Williams. Copyright © 1983 by Vera B. Williams.

Harcourt Brace & Company: Cover illustration from *On the Day You Were Born* by Debra Frasier. Copyright © 1991 by Debra Frasier. Pronunciation Key from *HBJ School Dictionary*, Third Edition. Text copyright © 1990 by Harcourt Brace & Company.

HarperCollins Publishers: Cover illustration from *Chanticleer and the Fox* by Geoffrey Chaucer, adapted and illustrated by Barbara Cooney. Copyright © 1958 by Thomas Y. Crowell Company, Inc. Cover illustration by Ruth Lercher Bornstein from *Mama One, Mama Two* by Patricia MacLachlan. Illustration copyright © 1982 by Ruth Lercher Bornstein. Cover illustration by Alexander Pertzoff from *Three Names* by Patricia MacLachlan. Illustration copyright © 1991 by Alexander Pertzoff.

Holiday House: Cover illustration by Dick Gackenbach from *My Dog and the Green Sock Mystery* by David A. Adler. Illustration copyright © 1986 by Dick Gackenbach. Cover illustration from *The Bunny Play* by Loreen Leedy. Copyright © 1988 by Loreen Leedy. Cover illustration by Stephen Gammell from *Dancing Teepees: Poems of American Indian Youth*, selected by Virginia Driving Hawk Sneve. Illustration copyright © 1989 by Stephen Gammell.

Houghton Mifflin Company: Cover illustration by Peggy Fortnum from *A Bear Called Paddington* by Michael Bond. Copyright © 1958 by Michael Bond; copyright renewed © 1986 by Michael Bond. Cover illustration from *The Bicycle Man* by Allen Say. Copyright © 1982 by Allen Say.

Alfred A. Knopf, Inc.: Cover illustration by Thomas B. Allen from *Blackberries in the Dark* by Mavis Jukes. Illustration copyright © 1985 by Thomas B. Allen.

Little, Brown and Company: Cover illustration by Leslie Baker from *All Those Secrets of the World* by Jane Yolen. Illustration copyright © 1991 by Leslie Baker.

Little, Brown and Company, in association with Arcade Publishing, Inc: *Good Morning, River!* by Lisa Westberg Peters. Text copyright © 1990 by Lisa Westberg Peters.

Lodestar Books, an affiliate of Dutton Children's Books, a division of Penguin Books USA Inc.: "The Case of the Earthenware Pig" from *Encyclopedia Brown Solves Them All* by Donald J. Sobol. Text copyright © 1968 by Donald J. Sobol.

Lothrop, Lee & Shepard Books, a division of William Morrow & Company, Inc.: Cover illustration by Jim LaMarche from *Mandy* by Barbara D. Booth. Illustration copyright © 1991 by Jim LaMarche. Cover illustration by Ed Young from *Eyes of the Dragon* by Margaret Leaf. Illustration copyright © 1987 by Ed Young. Cover illustration by Barbara Cooney from *Roxaboxen* by Alice McLerran. Illustration copyright © 1991 by Barbara Cooney.

Macmillan Publishing Company, a Division of Macmillan, Inc.: Cover illustration by Hans Helweg from *The Tales of Olga da Polga* by Michael Bond. Copyright © 1971 by Michael Bond. Cover illustration from *I Have Another Language: The Language Is Dance* by Eleanor Schick. Copyright © 1992 by Eleanor Schick.

Margaret K. McElderry Books, an imprint of Macmillan Publishing Company: Cover illustration by Wendy Smith from *Making Friends* by Margaret Mahy. Illustration copyright © 1990 by Wendy Smith.

Morrow Junior Books, a division of William Morrow & Company, Inc.: Cover illustration by Louis Darling from *Henry and the Paper Route* by Beverly Cleary. Copyright © 1957 by Beverly Cleary. Cover illustration by Kay Life from *Muggie Maggie* by Beverly Cleary. Illustration copyright © 1990 by William Morrow & Company, Inc. Cover illustration by Alan Tiegreen from *Ramona Forever* by Beverly Cleary. Illustration copyright 1984 by William Morrow & Company, Inc. Cover illustration by Diane de Groat from *Aldo Peanut Butter* by Johanna Hurwitz. Illustration copyright © 1990 by Diane de Groat.

G. P. Putnam's Sons: Cover illustration from *The Art Lesson* by Tomie dePaola. Copyright © 1989 by Tomie dePaola.

Random House, Inc.: Cover illustration by Dora Leder from *Julian's Glorious Summer* by Ann Cameron. Illustration copyright © 1987 by Dora Leder.

Scholastic Inc.: "Benjamin Banneker's Wooden Clock" by Margaret Goff Clark from *Instructor's Read-Aloud Anthology*. Text copyright © 1984 by The Instructor Publications, Inc.

Simon & Schuster Books for Young Readers, New York: Cover illustration from *A Very Young Musician* by Jill Krementz. © 1991 by Jill Krementz.

Tambourine Books, a division of William Morrow & Company, Inc.: Cover illustration by Frané Lessac from *Caribbean Carnival* by Irving Burgie. Illustration copyright © 1992 by Frané Lessac.

Some of the authors' comments in this publication were taken from *Something About the Author*, edited by Anne Commire. Published by Gale Research Company and included by permission.